THE *Path* TO
Awakening

THE *Path* TO *Awakening*

How Buddhism's Seven Points of
Mind Training Can Lead You to a Life
of Enlightenment and Happiness

SHAMAR RINPOCHE

Edited and translated by Lara Braitstein

DELPHINIUM BOOKS

Harrison, New York • Encino, California

THE PATH TO AWAKENING
Copyright © 2014 by Lara Braitstein

Previous editions of this book were published in India by
Motilal Banarsidass (New Delhi) in 2009 and 2011

First Delphinium Books Edition 2014

Book design by Greg Mortimer

Library of Congress Cataloguing-in-Publication Data is available on request.

ISBN 978-1-88-328559-3

14 15 16 17 18 RRD 10 9 8 7 6 5 4 3 2

List of Illustrations

Figure 1: Avalokiteshvara, the bodhisattva of compassion (p25)
Figure 2: Atisha (p32)
Figure 3: Shakyamuni Buddha (p71)

Contents

Translator's Introduction

Atisha (982-1054 C.E.) is one of those rare characters in Tibetan history about whom there is no controversy. He is universally respected and remembered for his many contributions to the revitalization of Buddhism in Tibet at the outset of the Tibetan Renaissance (950-1200 C.E.) and those very contributions still have a crucial place in every school of Tibetan Buddhism. Among the most enduring aspects of his legacy was his introduction to the Tibetan religious sphere of the teachings that came to be called *lojong*, or Mind Training. Lojong teachings function to profoundly transform the practitioner's mind by training it in the practice of compassion and the development of wisdom. Both practical and profound, these teachings have not lost their popularity or their relevance despite the dramatic changes to their cultural context over the course of the past one thousand years.

As one would expect from such an intellectually inclined society, there has been an extraordinary proliferation of Tibetan lojong literature since Atisha's time. It has taken shape in lists of pithy aphorisms, poems, and prose commentaries. Some elements remain consistent, such as Chekawa Yeshé Dorjé's (1101-1175 C.E.) distillation of Atisha's teachings into seven points. Spread between the points is a series of root lines whose origins are themselves attributed to Atisha. Despite that attribution, there is nonetheless a surprising amount of variety in their arrangement and even content between lojong texts. An examination of various root texts reveals that adjusting the root lines is, in fact, something of a time-honoured tradition among lojong teachers who make these alterations in order to reflect their own understanding of the teachings and their own understanding of what constitutes the most pedagogically efficient method of transmitting those teachings. Consistent with the still-thriving intellectual and religious culture of the Tibetans, the production of lojong literature continues to this day. It was therefore with tremendous excitement that I accepted the invitation of H.H. the 14th Shamar Rinpoche to translate his own arrangement of the root lines and detailed commentary on Chekawa Yeshé Dorjé's Seven Points of Mind Training. I am extremely grateful for having had this opportunity to closely study the work of such a talented teacher, and to begin to understand how the literature and practice of lojong have developed throughout the past millennium by working with a great Lama on a new lojong commentary in the present.

I hope that readers will enjoy Shamar Rinpoche's Mind Training text *The Path to Awakening* as much as I have. As with any work of translation, errors and misunderstandings may occur. I apologize to Shamar Rinpoche and to the readers of this book for any mistakes.

This book could not have been completed without the help and support of a great number of people. I would like to thank a few of you in particular (though I am surely leaving out a few crucial people, I apologize in advance): Terry Burt, Chris Fang, Carol Gerhardt, Derek Hanger, Philippe Jedar, Thule G. Jug, Neeraj Khatri Chettri, Bart Mendel, Shahin Parhami, Dominique Thomas, Madeline J. Watson, Pamela Gayle White, and Sylvia Wong. Thanks to all of you for putting time and effort into making this book the best it could be.

Lara Braitstein
McGill University, 2009

A Note on Transliteration

Since the intended readership of this text is a general audience, Sanskrit terms have been written in phonetic form. This may be frustrating for readers who are familiar with Sanskrit, so this glossary of terms provides correct transliteration for key terms that have been altered for ease of pronunciation.

Sanskrit Terms

Avalokiteshvara	*Avalokiteśvara*
Atisha	*Atiśa*
Atisha Dipamkara Srijnana	*Atiśa Dīpaṁkara Śrījñāna*
bhumi	*bhūmi*
dharmakaya	*dharmakāya*
maha	*mahā*
Mahayana	*mahāyāna*
Nagarjuna	*Nāgārjuna*
nirmanakaya	*nirmāṇakāya*
nirvana	*nirvāṇa*
paramita	*pāramitā*
Rajagrha	*Rājagṛha*
sambhogakaya	*saṁbhogakāya*
samsara	*saṁsāra*
Shakyamuni	*Śākyamuni*
shamatha	*śamatha*
Shantideva	*Śāntideva*
shravaka	*śrāvaka*
shunyata	*śūnyatā*
sutra	*sūtra*
sambhogakaya	*Saṁbhogakāya*
svabhavikakaya	*svabhāvikakāya*
trisvabhava	*trisvabhāva*
vipashyana	*vipaśyanā*

The Buddha's Teachings:
An Introduction

The Buddha of our era, Shakyamuni, delivered teachings nearly continuously for the 45 years that he lived after attaining full awakening. Many sentient beings benefited from his teachings, and the works of his we have now have been passed down from the time of his direct followers to us. In fact he gave many different kinds of teachings using many different methods, and he didn't only teach human beings. The power of awakening is such that one's compassion allows one to manifest simultaneously in as many different forms as will allow one to reach any being who is present. Anyone, human, animal, semi-human, or divine, who has the right karmic background will perceive the body and speech of a Buddha in a form that is familiar and pleasing to them. For example, we humans have one head, two arms, two legs, etc. and when Buddha lived and taught in human society he was perceived in human form. But sentient beings are not the same everywhere. There may be a realm where living beings are hollow and have no organs inside their bodies, where they have four heads and arms, or communicate without moving their mouth or making sounds. If such beings were to attend the Buddha's teachings, Buddha would appear in their form, and his speech would not be in this world's human language, they would instead hear it in their own language. That is the power of awakening.

Despite their incredible vastness, the Buddha's teachings, or *dharma,* can be divided into three collections or subjects. These are also referred to as the three turnings of the wheel of the dharma. Two of these turnings of the wheel are associated with a specific time and place, and the last one is more generalized. The first turning of the wheel took place in present-day Sarnath, close to Varanasi, when the Buddha gave his very first teachings after his awakening. He taught five human disciples—formerly fellow ascetics—and to a host of heavenly and semi-human beings who gathered to hear his teachings but who the five humans could not perceive. The second turning of the wheel was in present-day Rajgir (known then as Rajagriha) where Buddha taught many *arhats,* his most advanced disciples, among whom were *bodhisattvas* like Manjushri who were still in human form. In addition, there were again innumerable heavenly beings in attendance. The third turning of the wheel does not have a specific time, place or audience associated with it. Instead it is understood to have taken place continuously throughout Buddha's life.

The first turning of the wheel consisted of teachings

aimed principally at taming the body, speech and mind. The second turning of the wheel was mainly teachings that pointed to deep *samadhis*, or states of profound meditative absorption. The third turning of the wheel consisted of teachings based on the Three Natures (*trisvabhava* in Sanskrit): the Imagined Nature, which is the dualistic division of experience into self and other; the Dependent Nature, which is the undivided flow of experience; and the Perfected Nature, which is the Dependent Nature free of the Imagined Nature. The profound teachings on the Three Natures open the door to the many vast qualities of wisdom that do not manifest themselves easily and are not obvious to the untrained observer.

After Buddha's lifetime the qualified interpreters of his dharma, the *Mahapanditas* or Great Learned Ones, classified all his teachings into three vehicles. The first vehicle is characterized by the fact that it revolves around the teachings on no-self (*anatman*). In this vehicle, the view is *no-self* and the practice consists of meditation on it. The conduct of practitioners in this vehicle is supported by the monastic code of discipline, the *vinaya*. That code of discipline includes strict celibacy. In fact, sex is the cause of rebirth—both in terms of being the means of reproduction, and in terms of planting the seeds in your mind that result in *your own* rebirth. By renouncing that cause of rebirth and by following the direct path of meditation, a practitioner will achieve the full realization of no-self.

The second and third vehicles are both for bodhisattvas, practitioners who are bound by their altruistic intention to help all sentient beings. The view of both these vehicles is *shunyata*, or emptiness: the understanding that the world as we experience it divided into subject and object, perceiver and perceived, does not really exist as such. Because everything we experience does not have inherent existence, this opens the possibility that anything can happen. The meditation employed by both the second and third vehicles allows you to experience that view of emptiness, and trains you to then use the illusions of sentient beings for their own benefit. In that way you can use the illusion of dualistic appearances for something positive. In fact you can learn to take better rebirths over and over in the realms of sentient beings in order to be helpful. The merit generated by continuously helping others in more and more skillful ways is like a limitless storehouse of treasure that will eventually result in perfect enlightenment. That state is the most helpful and productive of all. The difference between the second and third vehicles is a matter of emphasis. In the second vehicle, there are many teachings on emptiness; whereas in the third vehicle the teachings revolve more around what arises out of emptiness. The third vehicle is in fact useful for every kind of practitioner: the *shravakas* or "listeners", the *pratyekabuddhas* or solitary realizers, and for bodhisattvas.

In order to achieve awakening, studying these subjects is not enough. To reach the goal you also need the key. The key is the essential instructions to unlock the heart of the teachings. Each practice has a key that is not always openly explained. The key is held by those few serious practitioners who were taught it by the long line of the most experienced meditation teachers. In fact there are four kinds of teachers. There are those scholars who have no key, there are teachers who have key instructions but no scholarly training or ability, there are teachers who are both key holders and scholars, and of course there are also some teachers who have no key or scholarly training! Among the four, only the last needs to be completely avoided, and for the rest it really boils down to understanding how trustworthy a teacher is regardless of the subject or vehicle.

If you only follow the dharma that is explained in a scholarly way, that is good. To only follow key instructions without scholarly training is very good. If you follow both the scholarly training and the key instructions, that is supremely good. It perhaps goes without saying that having neither scholarly access to the dharma nor key instructions does zero good! But in any case, to reach the goal you need the key.

There are also four types of students who are suitable disciples for these different teachers. For a general audience in need of the most basic introduction, the type of teacher who is only trained as a scholar is great. For very advanced practitioners engaging in intense practice, the teacher who only holds key instructions is great. Finally, the combined scholar/keyholder is perfectly suited for any type or level of student. The fourth type of teacher, the one with neither scholarly training nor key instructions, is in fact perfect for nobody. Ironically, it is also the type of teacher that many may be tempted to follow!

Root Text

Introduction

Mind Training, or *lojong*, is a comprehensive practice that is suitable for all types of students. It contains the entire path and does not depend on a person's background or sectarian affiliation. Put into practice diligently, it is enough to lead you all the way to awakening.

The Seven Points of Mind Training were originally devised by Chekawa to give condensed notes to his disciples, something to allow them to remember the core of his most important instructions. Over time, different teachers have given their own commentaries on the Seven Points. Some of these have been written down, and some have been transmitted orally since Chekawa's time. Readers who are familiar with Mind Training texts will have noticed that the slogans that fill out the Seven Points vary from root text to root text. It is traditional that many teachers who transmit the Seven Points will make some decisions about the order and content of the slogans. Some versions are longer than ohters, some more complex than others, but all of them carry the power and simplicity of Chekawa's Seven Points, which themselves do not vary.

What follows this introduction is a root text of this teaching on Mind Training, in both Tibetan and English. It consists of Chekawa's Seven Points of Mind Training, together with many slogans that function as a kind of condensed commentary, and in between these are my own additional notes making the organization of the root text clear. Following the root text, the rest of this book is my own detailed commentary on the Points and slogans.

The Seven Points elucidated by Chekawa can be divided into four steps: the preliminaries, cultivation of superior view meditation (Sanskrit: *vipashyana*; Tibetan: *lhaktong*), the meditation of giving and taking (Tibetan: *tonglen*), and the causes and conditions for developing giving and taking. As will be explained in detail below, the preliminaries consist of a basic understanding of the Buddha's teachings and developing a stable mind through *shiné*, or calm abiding meditation (Sanskrit: *shamatha*). After that, insight into emptiness and the unborn nature of mind is accomplished through the meditation of superior view, known as *vipashyana* in Sanskrit. Then comes the main practice, tonglen, or giving and taking. One who is diligent and accomplished in the practice of tonglen can even achieve the first bodhisattva level, or *bhumi*, within a single lifetime. Mind Training is a practice that nurses and cultivates the Buddha Nature, that pure seed of awakening that is at the very heart of every sentient being. It has the power to transform even egotistical self-clinging into selflessness.

For this reason, Mind Training practitioners say that self-clinging has the Buddha Nature. Its very nature is selflessness. Finally, the fourth step is understanding the causes and conditions required to accomplish tonglen.

Originally this was written as a curriculum for the Bodhi Path Centers that I have founded throughout North America, Asia and Europe. My goal is to encourage effective, transformative practice that does not depend on sectarian divisions. For this reason, I consider this curriculum to be completely *rimé*, or non-sectarian, and consider the Bodhi Path Centers to be nonsectarian as well.

While Tibetan Buddhism already has strong roots outside Tibet, there is really no benefit to be had from maintaining the rigid sectarian divisions that were so much a part of Buddhism in Tibet itself. Tibetans can benefit from being less sectarian, and certainly non-Tibetans have no need for such distinctions.

PREFACE TO THE ROOT TEXT

དེ་ཡང་། ་་་ བློ་སྦྱོང་དོན་བདུན་མའི་རྩ་བའི་ཚིག་བཅད་རྣམས་ལ་མི་འདྲ་བ་

དུ་མ་ཞིག་འདུག་ཅིང་ཅུང་ཟད་འཛུག་མི་བདེ་བས། ་་་དོན་བདུན་མའི་

འགྲེལ་པ་གདམས་ངག་མཛོད་ནང་དུ་བཞུགས་པ་དང་། ་་་གཞན་ཡང་།

ཞུ་དར་ལྷ་པ། ་་་དངུལ་ཆུ་ཐོགས་མེད། ་་་ཀུན་མཁྱེན་ཏཱ་ར་ན་ཐ།

བློ་གྲོས་མཐའ་ཡས་བཅས་ཀྱིས་མཛད་པའི་འགྲེལ་པ་སོགས་དཔྱད་གཞི་བྱས་མ་ཐར།

ཁོ་བོ་ཉིད་ནར་ཁྲི་འཛིན་ཆོས་ཀྱི་བློ་གྲོས་པས་སྤྱག་སྟར་གསོལ་འདེབས་དང་གཉན་

བ་ཞུས་སྟེ། ་་་རང་གི་རིགས་འཛུག་ཚོ་གདམས་ངག་ཐབ་མོ་འདི་ལ་ཇི་བཞིན་

འཛུག་པདེའི་ཆེད་དུ་ཁོ་ནར་དམིགས་ནས། ་་་འདས་ལོ ༢༠༢༤ མེ་ཕག་ལོའི་

ཟླ་བ་ ༩ ཚེས ༡ ་་་ སྤྱི་ལོ ༢༠༠༢ ཟླ་བ་ ༦ ་་་ ཆེས ༡ ༤ ཉིན་རྩ་ཆེག་

འདི་བཞིན་བསྒྲིགས་སྟེ་བཏུན་འབེབས་བྱས་པར་ནོངས་འགལ་མཆིས་ཚ

ཕྱགས་གནུ་བོར་བཞུགས་པའི་མཁས་དབང་རྣམས་ལ་བཟོད་གསོལ་ཕུལ།

Because there are many different versions of the root text of the Seven Points of Mind Training, I became concerned that this would be confusing for practitioners. As this was clearly a subject to be analyzed, I studied many commentaries: the commentary on the Seven Points found in the *Dam Ngak Dzö*, the fifth Shamarpa's commentary, Ngulchu Tokme's commentary, omniscient Taranatha's commentary, the commentary of Jamgön Lodrö Thayé, and more. Finally, I, Shamarpa Chökyi Lodrö, receiving the permission of my own yidam, solely for the purpose of making these profound instructions easier for my followers to understand, on the first day of the third month of the Fire Pig Year (2134); the 18th day the fourth month of the western year 2007, decided to reorganize the root verses like this. If there are any mistakes here, I apologize to the learned ones in all directions.

ROOT TEXT   ༄༅། །ཐུགས་རྗེ་ཆེན་པོ་ལ་ཕྱག་འཚལ་ལོ།

བརྒྱུད་ཁྱུངས་བཅའ་བར་བསྨན་པ་ནི།

མན་ངག་བདུད་རྩིའི་སྙིང་པོ་འདི། གསེར་གླིང་པ་ནས་བརྒྱུད་པ་ཡིན།

ཆེ་བ་བསྟན་པ་ནི།

སྐྱེགས་མ་ལུ་པོ་བདོ་བ་འདི། བྱང་ཆུབ་ལམ་དུ་བསྒྱུར་བ་ཡིན།

རྗེ་རྗེ་ཉི་མ་ལྷོན་ཤིང་བཞིན། གཞུང་དོན་ལ་སོགས་ཤེས་པར་བྱ།

❀   དོན་དང་པོ་སྦྱིན་འགྲོ་བསྐུན་ཅིང་དེ་ཡང་འདོར་གསུམ་མི་དམིགས་པར་བསྒོམ་པ་ནི།

དང་པོ་སྦྱིན་འགྲོ་དག་ལ་བསྒོམ། ཆོས་རྣམས་རྨི་ལམ་ལྱུ་བྱུར་བསམ།

❀   དོན་གཉིས་པ་བྱང་ཆུབ་སེམས་གཉིས་སྐྱོང་བའི་མན་ངག་ཐོག་མར་དོན་དམ་བྱང་ཆུབ་སེམས་ནི།

མ་སྐྱེས་རིག་པའི་གཉིས་ལ་དཔྱད། གཉེན་པོ་ང་ཉེ་སྙིན་ལ་སྒྲུད།

གཉེན་པོ་ཉིད་ཀྱང་རང་སར་གྲོལ། ཏི་བོ་ཀུན་གཞིའི་ངང་ལ་བཞག།

ཐུན་མཚམས་རྒྱུ་མའི་སྐྱེས་བྱུར་བྱ། འདྲས་བུའི་རེ་བ་ཐམས་ཅད་སྤངས།

གཉིས་པ་ཀུན་རྫོབ་དང་དོན་དམ་བྱང་ཆུབ་ཀྱི་སེམས་ཟུང་འཇུག་ཏུ་སྐྱོང་བའི་མན་ངག་ནི།

གཏོང་ལེན་གཉིས་པོ་སྤེལ་མར་སྒྲུང། དེ་གཉིས་རླུང་ལ་བསྐྱོན་པར་བྱ།

ཡུལ་གསུམ་དུག་གསུམ་དགེ་རྩ་གསུམ། སྐྱོང་ལམ་ཀུན་ཏུ་ཚིག་གིས་སྒྲུང།

❀   དོན་གསུམ་པ་རྐྱེན་ངན་བྱང་ཆུབ་ཀྱི་ལམ་དུ་བསྒྱུར་བའི་མན་ངག་ལ་གཉིས་ སྟོང་དང་ཁྱད་པར་ཅན་གཉིས་ལས་དང་པོ་ནི།

སྐྱོན་བཅུད་སྐྱིག་པས་གང་བའི་ཚེ། རྐྱེན་ངན་བྱང་ཆུབ་ལམ་དུ་བསྒྱུར།

གཉིས་པ་ལ་ཁྱད་པར་ཅན་གསུམ་ལས་དང་པོ་ཀུན་རྗོབ་བྱང་ཆུབ་སེམས་ཀྱི་རྐྱེན་ངན་བྱང་ཆུབ་ཀྱི་ལམ་དུ་བསྒྱུར་བའི་མན་ངག་ནི།

ལེ་ལན་ཐམས་ཅད་གཅིག་ལ་བདའ། ཀུན་ལ་བཀའ་དྲིན་ཆེ་བར་བསྒོམ།

གཉིས་པ་དོན་དམ་བྱང་ཆུབ་སེམས་ཀྱིས་ཉེན་པར་བྱང་ཆུབ་ཀྱི་ལམ་དུ་སྦྱོང་བའི་མན་ངག་ནི།

འཁྲུལ་སྣང་སྐྱུ་བཞིར་སྐྱོམ་པ་ཡི། སྣང་ཉིད་བསྲུང་བ་བྲ་ན་མེད།

ལྷ་བ་གསུམ་དང་ནམ་མཁའ་མཚོད། རྣལ་འབྱོར་སྲུང་བ་བྲ་ན་མེད།

གསུམ་པ་སྦྱོར་བ་ཁྲག་པར་ཅན་གྱིས་ཉེན་པར་བྱང་ཆུབ་ཀྱི་ལམ་དུ་སྦྱོང་བའི་མན་ངག་ནི།

སྦྱོར་བ་བཞི་ལྡན་ཐབས་ཀྱི་མཚོག །འཕུལ་ལ་གང་ཕྱུག་སློམ་དུ་སྐྱུར།

༄ དོན་བཞི་པ་ཚ་གཅིག་གི་ཉམས་ལེན་དྲིལ་ནས་བསྟན་པའི་མན་ངག་ནི།

མན་ངག་སྙིང་པོ་མདོར་བསྡུས་པ། སློབས་ལྷ་དག་དང་སྒྱུར་བར་བྱ།

ཐེག་ཆེན་འཕོ་བའི་གདམས་ངག་ནི། སློབས་ལྷ་ཉིད་ཡིན་སློང་ལམ་གཅེས།

༄ དོན་ལྷ་པ་རྟོ་འབྱོངས་པའི་ཚད་བསྟན་པ་ནི།

ཚོས་ཀུན་ད་གོས་པ་གཅིག་ཏུ་འདུས། དཔང་པོ་གཉིས་ཀྱི་གཙོ་བོ་བཟུང་།

ཡིད་བདེ་འབའ་ཞིག་རྒྱུན་དུ་བསྐྱེན། ཡེངས་ཀྱང་ཐུབ་ན་འབྱངས་པ་ཡིན།

༄ དོན་དྲུག་པ་བློ་སློང་གི་དམ་ཚིག་བསྟན་པ་ནི།

སྤྱི་དོན་གསུམ་ལ་རྟག་ཏུ་བསླབ། འདུན་པ་བསྒྱུར་ལ་རང་སོར་བཞག །

ཡན་ལག་ཉམས་པ་བརྗོད་མི་བྱ། གཞན་ཕྱོགས་གང་ཡང་མི་བསམ་མོ།

དུག་ཅན་གྱི་ཟས་སྤང་། གཞུང་བཟང་པོ་མ་བསྟེན། ཕག་དན་མ་གོད།

འཕྲང་མ་སྒུགས། གནད་ལ་མི་དབབ། མཛོ་ཁལ་གླང་ལ་མི་འགྲོ།

མགྱོགས་ཀྱི་རྩེ་མི་གཏོད། ལྷོ་ལྷོག་མི་བྱ། ལྷ་བདུད་དུ་མི་དབབ།

ཀུན་ལ་བྲན་གྱི་ཐ་མ་ལྟར་བྱ། སྐྱིད་ཀྱི་ཡན་ལག་ཏུ་སྲུག་མ་ཚོལ།

༈ དོན་བདུན་པ་བློ་སྦྱོང་གི་བསླབ་བྱ་བསྐུལ་བ་ནི།

རྣལ་འབྱོར་ཐམས་ཅད་གཅིག་གིས་བྱ།   ལོག་གནོན་ཐམས་ཅད་གཅིག་གིས་བྱ།

ཐོག་མཐའ་གཉིས་ལ་བྱ་བ་གཉིས།   གཉིས་པོ་གང་བྱུང་བཟོད་པར་བྱ།

གཉིས་པོ་སྲོག་དང་གདོས་ནས་བསྲུང་།   དཀའ་བ་གསུམ་ལ་བསླབ་པར་བྱ།

རྒྱུ་ཡི་གཙོ་བོ་རྣམ་གསུམ་བླང་།   ཉམས་པ་མེད་པ་རྣམ་གསུམ་བསྒོམ།

འབྲལ་མེད་གསུམ་དང་ལྡན་པར་བྱ།   ཡུལ་ལ་ཕྱོགས་མེད་དག་ཏུ་སྒོམ།

ཁྱབ་དང་གཏིང་འབྱོངས་ཀུན་ལ་གཅེས།   བཀོལ་བ་རྣམས་ལ་རྟག་ཏུ་བསྒོམ།

རྐྱེན་གཞན་དག་ལ་བློས་མི་བྱ།   ད་རེས་གཙོ་བོ་ཉམས་སུ་བླངས།   གོ་ལོག་མི་བྱ།

རེས་འཇོག་མི་བྱ།   དོལ་ཆོད་སྒྲུང་།   རྟོག་དཔྱོད་གཉིས་ཀྱིས་ཐར་བར་བྱ།

ཡུས་མ་བསྒོམ།   གོ་ལོང་མི་སྦོམ།   ཡུད་ཚམ་པ་མི་བྱ།   ཨོར་ཆེ་མ་འདོད།

མཛད་པ་པོའི་གདིངས་བརྗོད་པས་གཞན་ལ་དཔལ་འབྱེད་པ་ནི།

བདག་ཉིད་མོས་པ་མང་བའི་རྒྱས།   སྡུག་བསྔལ་གཏད་ངན་ཁྱད་བསད་ནས།

བདག་འཛིན་འདུལ་བའི་གདམས་ངག་ལས།   ད་ནི་ཤི་ཡང་མི་འགྱོད་དོ།

ROOT TEXT

Homage to the Great Compassionate One!

Instructions on the lineage:
This is the key instruction,
the essential nectar generated by Serlingpa.

How great the practice is:
The five degenerations are happening now;
You should convert them into the path of awakening.
Like the diamond, the sun, the medicinal tree,
it is the principal, ever precious discipline.

**First Point: Learn the preliminaries;
Furthermore, be trained in not conceptualizing
the three spheres.**
First, train in the preliminaries;
think that all phenomena are like a dream.

**Second Point: Key instructions for training in the two
bodhicittas, beginning with ultimate bodhicitta:**
Analyze the unborn nature of mind.
Purify the strongest negative emotion first.
Even the remedy naturally liberates itself.
Rest in the essence of mind, the basis of everything.
In post meditation, know that all phenomena are illusory.
Abandon all hope for results.

Second, the instructions on training in the union
of conventional and ultimate bodhicitta:
Practice alternately the two, giving and taking.
Place the two upon the breath.
Three objects, three poisons, three roots of virtue.
Train your conduct by means of the slogans.

Third Point: Convert adversities into the path of awakening.

Among ordinary and extraordinary instructions,
begin with the first:
When beings and the world are filled with evil, convert
adversities into the path of awakening.

Second, among the three extraordinary instructions,
the first is how conventional bodhicitta is used
to convert adversities into the path of awakening:
Hold one fault accountable for all misfortunes.
Reflect on the great kindness of all beings.

The second is how ultimate bodhicitta is used
to transform adversities into the path of awakening:
Cultivate deluded appearance as the Four Kayas;
Emptiness is the unsurpassed protection.
Three views are like the treasury of the sky,
the unsurpassed protection of the yoga.

The third is the extraordinary instruction
to convert adversities into the path of awakening:
Mastering the four practices is the supreme method.
Whatever you encounter in the present,
use it in your meditation.

Fourth Point: Implement Mind Training in this life.
The instructions condensed into their essence:
Train in the five powers.
The Great Vehicle teachings on death are the
five powers themselves; your conduct is critical.

Fifth Point: The measure of Mind Training.
All dharma teachings are for a single purpose.
Rely on the better of the two witnesses.
Be sustained continuously by a joyful mind.
You are well trained if you can even withstand distraction.

Sixth Point: Commitments of Mind Training.
Always abide by the three basic principles.
Remaining natural, transform your attitude.
Do not talk about the defects of others.
Whatever the faults of others may be, do not
contemplate them.
Abandon poisonous food.
Helping others is not based on returning favors.
Do not expose the faults of others to irritate them.

Do not wait in ambush.
Never strike at the heart.
Do not put an ox's load on a cow.
Do not aim to be the best.
Do not misuse the remedy.
Do not use gods for evil.
Be like a humble servant before all.
Do not delight in the suffering of others.

Seventh Point: Advice for Mind Training.
Practice all yogas in one way.
Subdue all obstacles by one method.
Two actions to perform: at the beginning and at the end.
Be patient with whichever of the two arises.
Guard the two even at the cost of your life.
Train in the three difficulties.
Keep the three main causes.
Cultivate the three without diminishment.
Make the three inseparable.
Practice with impartiality.
All training must be pervasive and profound.
Meditate consistently in every circumstance.
Do not depend on external conditions.
From now on, practice is the chief priority.
Do not be misdirected.
Do not be inconsistent.
Train uninterruptedly.

Liberate by examination and analysis.
Do not seek recognition.
Do not hold on to anger.
Do not be moody.
Do not seek gratitude.

*Chekawa explains that now he has the
necessary confidence and will to encourage others:*

*Through my great intention and resolve,
I ignored my own suffering and ill repute,
And obtained the instructions to defeat my own ego clinging.
Now, I have no regrets even if I were to die this moment.*

*Homage to the Great
Compassionate One!*

Avalokiteshvara, the bodhisattva of compassion.
Thangka by Huei-Shion Tsai

Ja Chekawa Yeshé Dorjé, author of the root text, be-gins by paying homage to Avalokiteshvara, the great Awakening Being esteemed as the very embodiment of the compassion of all Buddhas.

Instructions on the lineage:
**This is the key instruction, the essential nectar
generated by Serlingpa.**

Now we come to the main subject: the Seven Points of
Mind Training. This is the key instruction of the Kadam
school, the lineage of which comes from Atisha Dipam-
kara Srijnana (982-1054 C.E.). Though of course this
key method comes from Buddha, for a long time it was
passed on as a secret oral tradition along a long lineage of
great bodhisattvas.

It is called *dütsi nyingpo*, or essential nectar. The nectar is a liquid so pure that even one drop can purify a
vast body of water. These instructions are like the very
essence of that purifying, healing nectar.

This nectar is not only able to purify the mind, but
when Atisha received these instructions he effectively purified the transmission of Buddhism as well. In the 11th
century, Buddhism slowly started declining in India. This
was exactly as Buddha had predicted. When he was teaching he repeatedly told his disciples that his teachings would
definitely disappear so it was critically important for them
to practice diligently immediately. At every *sojong* (cer-
emony for purifying monastic precepts), he repeated this
warning. So it happened that during Atisha's time there
began to be indications that this disappearance of the Buddha's teachings from India was starting to happen. For ex-

ample, during Atisha's life, the combined lineages of the
bodhisattva vow—the Maitreya-Asanga lineage and the
Nagarjuna lineage—had already disappeared from India.
Everybody was practicing one or the other, but not the two
together. As a great bodhisattva, Atisha saw that in the
future he could benefit beings in Tibet before Buddhism
declined in India. He understood that by sowing the seeds
of *buddhadharma* there, when it declined in India it would
live on in Tibet. For that reason, he went all the way to In-
donesia to meet Serlingpa, the only master who still held
that combined lineage of the bodhisattva vow.

The second son of a local king, Atisha was born in
an area along the border between present-day India and
Bangladesh. His parents named him Chandragarbha, the
Essence of the Moon. At the age of twenty he received
all the vinaya vows (monastic vows) and was named Di-
pamkara Srijnana. It was not until his more senior years,
during his teaching days in Tibet, that he became known
to the people there as Atisha.

Atisha traveled to Sumatra by ship on a journey that
took over a year. On the way he was faced with tremendous obstacles such as storms and aggressive sea creatures. At one point he was attacked by Maheshvara.
Maheshvara took the shape of a gigantic, terrifying monster and caused a treacherous storm to descend upon the
ship: lightning, thunder, huge waves and an enormous
whirlpool that very nearly caused the ship to sink. From

the midst of the whirlpool emerged the sea monster, threatening to devour all on board. Atisha established himself in a profound, stable meditation and generated compassion and loving kindness. The entreaties of Atisha's terrified travel companions combined with Atisha's tremendous merit caused Amrita Kundali, the wrathful Buddhist deity, to manifest and destroy the sea monster. In his wrath, lightning generated by Yamantaka also struck Pashupatinath (the ancient Shiva temple complex in Kathmandu), the Bön kingdom of Shangshung, and Mongol invaders who were bent on attacking Bodhgaya. Finally, overpowered by Atisha's love and Yamantaka's lightning, Maheshvara took the form of a young boy and begged forgiveness. Events like these plagued Atisha's journey, but in the end he was successful.

He eventually arrived in Sumatra and was given a warm welcome by Serlingpa, a prince in Sumatra who had become a great Buddhist master. Atisha, who was himself a prince, spent twelve years there and received all of Serlingpa's teachings, including, of course, his key instructions. The Mind Training teachings contained in this book are the very same key instructions, most especially the exchanging of self and other. It must be mentioned here that even today some things are kept hidden from all but the most serious practitioners. Here, when it comes to the teachings on ultimate *bodhicitta*, much will remain unwritten.

Before Atisha left to return to India, Serlingpa gave him six texts, which contained the condensed essence of the *Mahayana* (Great Vehicle). Atisha, being well versed in both the sutras and tantras (exoteric and esoteric teachings of the Buddha), realized that he had, in effect, been given the keys to the treasury of the Buddha's teachings. Atisha felt deeply grateful to his spiritual mentor and rejoiced in the good fortune of sentient beings. From then on, he always traveled with the six texts.

When Atisha was already sixty years old, the local kings in Tibet invited him to their country. After much convincing, Atisha traveled there to teach. The Tibetan prince, Jangchup Ö, impressed upon Atisha the urgent need to restore Buddhism, which had deteriorated in the land. Charlatans and magicians were misleading his people. The Prince asked Atisha to clear up the misconceptions and superstitions. He especially requested that the teachings be presented in simple layperson's terms for the benefit of the populace. From the six texts of Master Serlingpa, Atisha condensed the teachings. On a few pieces of paper, he wrote down 68 verses of the now famous: *A Lamp for the Path to Enlightenment* (*Bodhipathapradipa* in Sanskrit). The genre of teachings is also known as *Lam Rim* (Lam: path; Rim: stages), or *The Gradual Path to Enlightenment.*

One of two principal disciples of Atisha was Dromtönpa (1005-1064). Together, they translated Serlingpa's text, *The Wheel of Sharp Weapons that Effectively Strikes the Heart of the Foe*, from Sanskrit into Tibetan. At first, Atisha only taught Lam Rim to a select few disciples, of whom Dromtönpa was one. When Dromtönpa asked him why, Atisha replied that it was because only he was a worthy and qualified vessel.

After Atisha's death, Dromtönpa organized the transmissions he had received from his guru and started the lineage that came to be known as the Kadam. Mind Training was the very heart of these teachings. However, these Kadam teachings were mainly kept secret in the beginning, transmitted orally from master to disciple. From Dromtönpa, the lineage transmission passed to Potowa. From Potowa, the transmission passed to his two disciples, Langri Thangpa (1054-1123) and Sharawa (1070-1141). Chekawa (1101-1175), the author of our root text, received the transmission from Sharawa.

Born in a place called Lura in the southwestern part of Tibet, Chekawa first met a teacher called Loro Rechung. He later received his monastic vows from Tsarong Joten and Tsangdulwa, both Kadam lamas of Atisha's lineage. For the next four years, he studied and practiced. One day, Chekawa heard a disciple of Langri Thangpa reciting his master's Eight Verses for Training the Mind. What he heard was, *"I will learn to take on all defeat, and to offer all victories to others."* These words affected him so profoundly that he became determined to obtain the teachings. When he learned that the author of the verses had already passed away, he pressed on to find out who else would be able to teach him.

Chekawa then learned that it was Atisha who had introduced these teachings of the Buddha to Tibet. After learning about the illustrious lineage of teachers, most of whom had already passed away, Chekawa was relieved to discover that Sharawa was still alive. According to information given to him, Chekawa traveled to an area called Zho in central Tibet. There he found Master Sharawa and became his disciple. He remained there and studied with his spiritual teacher for six years. He then practiced for thirteen years, until all traces of selfishness in him had dissipated. Now a master of the Kadam lineage in his own right, Chekawa started to teach.

Chekawa passed away in the female wood sheep year (1175 C.E.) at the age of 75. He had accomplished his wish to practice, preserve and offer to as many people as possible these very precious lojong teachings.

Today, even though the Kadam lineage of Atisha's teachings is not considered a separate school in Tibetan Buddhism, it nevertheless forms an integral part of the lineage teachings of all four schools. This essential Mahayana practice has gained wide popularity in Tibet and as a result the collection of written works in Tibetan on lojong and Lamrim is now extensive.

Atisha
This thangka is attributed to Atisha himself.

Photo: Jigme Rinpoche; used courtesy of Karmapa Documentary Project

How great the practice is:
**The five degenerations are happening now; you should
convert them into the path of awakening.**

We are currently in the era of the five degenerations, a
time when the good eon is finishing. By "we" I am not
referring to our generation, or even to a time that includes a generation or two before our own. Our own eon
is the same as that of Shakyamuni Buddha: he himself
was also born and taught during this degenerate time.
The good eon had its own Buddhas, the first four. We
are most fortunate to have had a Buddha in this difficult
eon. For many, many generations, sentient beings have
lived and continue to live under very difficult conditions.
These adverse conditions have been termed "the five
degenerations", or the five crises. They are as prevalent
today as they were two thousand years ago:

Physical life: the human life span is limited to about
100 years. Even with the advances of modern medicine
and the availability of healthy foods, our lifespan is still
limited. Our physical bodies are susceptible to many dis-
eases that may cut our lives short.

The times: People are exposed to the precarious conditions of the environment that are the results of collective
karma. We are subject to many natural disasters that can
strike at any time, such as hurricanes, tornadoes, earth-
quakes, floods, fires, and sudden wars created by foolish
people.

Imperfect beings: Our current nature is not perfect. Even though we have the potential to develop in a positive way, we tend not to. The reason is that our many flaws (such as aggression) impede our chances to change for the better.

We live in a time when the majority of people are harming each other. We find ourselves in the midst of wars, violence, and exploitation. Many people suffer terrible atrocities at the hands of fellow humans. We are equally cruel to animals, and the animals also attack one another. The harm that living beings inflict upon each other is at its worst.

Wrong views: The trouble with wrong views is that they create many problems in the world. The imperfect views of the masses are rooted in ego grasping, confusion, and selfishness. These errors in thinking perpetuate injustice and harmful discrimination in society. Unfortunately, wrong views have found their way into all facets of life—in social, religious, cultural, political, and legal systems alike.

Disturbing emotions: People everywhere are dominated by negative emotions. In fact, disturbing emotions surface quite naturally all the time. Even though there are remedies for them, administering those remedies is rather an uphill battle. If we wish to develop even a tiny virtue, on the other hand, we have to exert great effort because most of the time the negative emotions simply overwhelm us.

We can observe that our own time is particularly bad. Nearly every single living being acts almost exclusively propelled by his or her afflicted mind. Most of the time, even the first impulse to act is grounded in afflicted mind and connected to bad karma. What we do, we do for our own good alone. Even those who try to do good in their lives, dharma practice or something else positive, will encounter many obstacles in life. Compare this to those who live dishonestly and are motivated by negativity, and we see that they do tend to live long and experience success. A terrible leader might be reelected, for example! In this dark time, there is almost no dharma method that can be a good remedy, except for the practice of exchanging self and other. So this key instruction of exchanging self and other is the only way that even the five degenerations can be used for the path to awakening. Once you know this, everything is useful. Even things that would usually be considered bad are suddenly good, and can be used towards a positive result. That also means that this method will overtake all bad karma, as well as the afflicted mental states and their consequences. It will all be taken over and used for enlightenment. Everything will be transformed, and you will find yourself falling into enlightenment.

**Like the diamond, the sun, the medicinal tree,
it is the principal, ever precious discipline.**

The Buddha gave many different teachings and instructions according to the abilities and propensities of his students. The methods vary in levels of difficulty and of accomplishment, but among the countless dharma practices, lojong is the superlative discipline. It is as priceless as a perfect diamond. Its worth cannot be measured because it is the very key that opens the inner door to enlightenment.

Another simile distinguishes the brilliance of lojong: these very precious teachings are said to shine as brightly as the sun itself. We have at our disposal all kinds of artificial light such as candlelight, gaslight, or electric light. But in the sun, all artificial lights are redundant. The sun completely dispels darkness and everything is shown clearly in its presence. Similarly, lojong clears away the ignorance of our mind and reveals everything as it is.

A third simile highlights the special power of lojong to accelerate our progress on the path: Mind Training is like the roots of a medicinal tree. The roots hold all the healing ingredients and these curative essences in turn permeate the entire tree: its trunk, branches and leaves, etc. Every single cell of the tree contains the medicines and we can harvest them through any of its parts. Similarly, Mind Training forms the best root for all dharma practice. When lojong has taken root in us, it imbues any practice we do with the same power to bring us swiftly to enlightenment.

By these three similes, you should understand, know, and remember the superior qualities of lojong which attest to its being the most valuable and meaningful practice in your life.

THE FIRST POINT

Learn the Preliminaries

The First Point: Learn the preliminaries; furthermore, be trained in not conceptualizing the three spheres.

Any explanation of the preliminary instructions must include an understanding of the purity of the three spheres. The three spheres are the agent, the object acted upon, and the action itself, and they must be understood to *not* be substantially real. In whatever actions one is instructed in, these three must not be conceptualized as truly existent. This will become more clear shortly.

First, train in the preliminaries; think that all phenomena are like a dream.

The first step toward awakening is taking refuge in the Three Jewels: the Buddha, the Dharma, and the Sangha. Before even taking that first step of taking the refuge vow, however, you must learn *the four thoughts that turn the mind towards enlightenment*: this precious human birth, impermanence, karma, and the defects of *samsara*. It is important to really reflect on them in order to gain lasting benefit. You have to understand the meaning of the Four Thoughts as they relate to you. What is their significance in your life *now*? See what difference they make when you reflect on them and apply them in everyday situations. In this way, you will begin to appreciate their qualities.

Detailed explanations of the Four Thoughts are readily available in many written works so here I will present only a very general discussion of them.

Precious Human Existence

The dharma teachings explain in detail what a precious human life is. It is by no means a mere generalization. Rather, the precious human life means precisely *you*. You can practice the dharma and so your life is precious: *you* have the freedom to pursue the dharma; *you* have time to attend dharma lectures; *you* have the intellect to understand the meaning; and *you* are physically able to do the practice. It makes you realize how lucky you are.

This traditional story provides a good metaphor for the preciousness of our human existence: a beggar once found a very large ruby on the road. He did not know he could get a lot of money in exchange for it. He went about every day begging for food when all the while the ruby sat in his pocket. In the end, he died a beggar. He did not use the ruby so it was worthless to him. This very simple story drives home the point that if you do not realize how inconceivably precious your life is now, it is as good as a ruby hidden in your pocket.

Impermanence

The thought of impermanence, the inevitability of transformation and death, changes how you relate to everything. It is important to be mindful of it. Passing moments become days, passing days become months, passing months become years, and passing years soon turn into the passing of our very lives. There are so many things we all want to experience and do in our lives, but so little of it gets accomplished. Think about how many years can go by without you even finishing one book you have set aside to read! Life is like that. It simply passes without you noticing. Since this particular life is so precious, we shouldn't waste our time following the whims of our wandering minds. Not knowing how long we will live and with no assurance of a good future rebirth, we must value the precious time we have right now and not waste it.

Karma

With respect to karma you should closely examine the causes and effects that show themselves in the different situations you face. Everything comes from a cause. Inasmuch as you understand that negative causes always produce negative results, you will resolve to act positively. Understanding how karmic seeds are planted and ripen can help to understand how karma works. Fundamentally, the deluded mind is the source of each life, and its experience of the particular realm it takes birth in is the illusion it projects. The experience of every moment and impression over the course of your life depends on your consciousness. The teachings explain that there is a separate consciousness for each sense organ: there is an eye-consciousness, an ear-consciousness, a tongue-consciousness, a nose-consciousness, and a body-consciousness (predominantly the sense of touch). Additionally there is a mind-consciousness. Everything you see depends on the functioning of your eye-consciousness, what you smell on your nose-consciousness etc. and what you *think* depends on your mind-consciousness. All the consciousnesses that support the physical sense organs report back, as it were, to the mind-consciousness, so visual, auditory, gustatory impressions are gathered by the consciousnesses of the sense organs and transmitted to the mind consciousness. The mind consciousness puts it all together as complete images, thoughts, concepts—every kind of mental object. The mind consciousness also contains the ground in which karmic seeds or impressions are planted. That is the ground of all. Negative seeds are planted by factors such as ignorance, egocentrism, pride, anger, envy, and hatred. Positive seeds are planted by such things as selflessness, compassion, and loving-kindness. These positive seeds produce results such as a precious human rebirth. How strong the results of any of these seeds are depends very much on how strong your intention is. Try to only think positively for a certain length of time and you will quickly realize how much more easily negative mental states arise than positive ones. It takes enormous will-power to think positively and no effort at all to let the mind dwell in negativity. Now think about how you and others have spontaneously and effortlessly been planting negative seeds in your mindstream since beginningless time. The negative seeds are innumerable, uncountable, and strong; they work like a pushy crowd shoving the positive mental states out of their way. This becomes especially pronounced after death, in the *bardo* (intermediate state) between the end of one life and the next rebirth. In that insecure and critical time before your next rebirth is secured, those pushy crowds of negative karma will elbow their way to the foreground of your experience and make things difficult. The powerful methods of Mind Training can eliminate those negative seeds, and this practice should be undertaken *now*, in *this* very precious human life. Without using those powerful methods, an opportunity as good as your present one may not come around again for billions of lifetimes.

The Defects of Samsara

While the unsatisfactory nature of samsara is self-evi-
dent if you reflect on it, nonetheless you have to convince
yourself to do so. We can think about samsara in terms
of the individual experience or as a collective experience.
We will begin with the individual. Every human being
on this earth longs for happiness. We all want as much
happiness as possible. What do we imagine happiness
comes from? In general, there is delicious food, romance,
sex, fame and power. The most unbelievably wealthy
man or woman on the planet *still* cannot do better than
good food, romance, fame and power. If we examine
where each of these leads us, the results are interesting.
Good food will eventually make you sick—heart disease,
diabetes, weight-gain, the list goes on. Romance inevitably depends on the emotions of your partner. Since each
individual has his or her own ego as well as a wealth
of negative emotions, romance never quite seems to last
long enough! You will eventually become dissatisfied
and fall into depression and anxiety. If you have the good
fortune to enjoy a long-lasting romance it will nevertheless come to an end when you get old and die. Fame always invites enemies because of the envy it elicits from
others. The life of a famous person is without freedom,
filled with discomfort, and bereft of privacy. There is no
ultimate goal to fame, there is only the precarious state

itself and its inevitable end. Power and privilege similarly create enemies. A life of power is a life of struggle:
the struggle to keep it, to protect it, and to not let it slip
away. It has no ultimate goal. Now one may ask oneself,
what, apart from these things, is good in samsara?

Let's examine the collective experience, beginning
with that of humans. Life is passing by every day. Your
life and the lives of others, be they friends, enemies, family, etc., are slipping away. This is the experience of the
human realm which we discussed above in more detail.
There are other realms to consider as well. There is the
samsaric experience of animals. Their experience is exactly what we see—they are always either attacking or
being attacked. Their lives are full of fear and suffering, and under the heavy weight of ignorance they lead
their lives and their lives end. They can only hope for
a better future rebirth. There are many other realms
as well that nearly connect to humans and animals but
are quite different, such as the life of the hungry ghosts,
those unfortunate beings who live constantly tormented
by thirst and hunger that can never be satisfied. There is
also the limitless suffering of beings in the hell-realms.
Somewhat contrary to this, there are also many beings
who are born in realms much more comfortable than our
own, such as gods and demi-gods. But that type of rebirth comes about solely on the basis of positive karma,
which, after it is exhausted, is jostled out of the way by

the pushy crowd of negative karma that will cause the fall of these beings into the hell realms after they die. Impermanence is inevitable and unavoidable, regardless of the realm you are born into. And you have been accumulating karma for as long as you have had ignorance and self-clinging—since beginningless time. Therefore, once you have found clear directions *out* of samsara you must not miss the opportunity!

If you train to integrate the Four Thoughts into your view, your understanding will deepen. Your commitment will follow accordingly. It is good to reflect on the biographies of the *mahabodhisattvas* (Atisha, Shantideva, Milarepa, for example) because their excellent qualities can inspire you to want to develop the same. For example, their great patience and resolve.

Once you have reflected sufficiently on these four thoughts, it is time to consider the qualities of the objects of refuge. Doing so plants very strong karmic seeds in the mind. Those wholesome seeds, reinforced by the power of taking refuge, will find their way to the very foreground of your life *in every lifetime*. In each and every life you will find your way to the teachings. For a profound reflection on the qualities of the Three Jewels, reading the Sutra of Recollecting the Qualities of the Three Jewels (*dkon mchog gsum rjes su dran pa'i mdo* in Tibetan) is the best. Here I will just give a brief explanation.

Buddha

When some benefit is gained, it is always twofold: for self and for other. Becoming a Buddha brings the highest benefit to oneself because you become fully enlightened. All ignorance is rooted out and you have fully attained the *dharmakaya* level, or the body of truth nature that is the timeless awakened wisdom of a Buddha. For others the benefit is equally magnificent: by manifesting the *sambhogakaya* and the *nirmanakaya*, the form bodies that fulfill the wishes and joys of all beings, a Buddha spontaneously and effortlessly helps and benefits others according to their needs. That is the state of Buddha. The ultimate benefit of taking refuge in the Buddha, therefore, is to plant the seeds of attaining Buddhahood yourself. The temporary, immediate benefit is that this seed of Buddhahood will allow you to accumulate all the merit necessary to attain awakening.

Dharma

The dharma is both the experience of realization and the Buddha's explanation through words. The meaning of the dharma is perfect, its wording is perfect, and it perfectly meets the needs of sentient beings on the path to awakening. When you take refuge in the dharma, the ultimate benefit is that the seed for being able to direct all sentient beings to Buddhahood with limitless, perfect power of speech is planted in your heart. You will provide extensive, unsurpassable instructions to all living beings. Indeed there is not a single phenomenon that cannot be explained by a Buddha. The temporary benefit is the merit of the dharma itself: in every life you will hear the dharma and you will understand it. You will never fall off the path to awakening.

Sangha

Sangha is the term used for the perfect community of practitioners. There are two: the ordinary sangha and the supreme sangha. The ordinary sangha isn't actually ordinary at all. The ordinary sangha consists of those who keep the vinaya discipline perfectly, all 253 vows. Their minds are well-trained in shiné (calm abiding meditation, shamatha in Sanskrit) and lhaktong (superior view meditation, vipashyana in Sanskrit) and they have the great motivation for awakening. Where there are four or more of them together, the complete merit potential of the sangha is there. This means that if someone offers anything to them, they gain the merit of offering to the perfect sangha even if they haven't yet attained a high level of realization.

The supreme, or uncommon sangha, is composed of those who have the two vows of bodhicitta, the altruistic intention, and who are deeply and skillfully practicing the six *paramitas* or perfections. This means that they are engaging in the perfect conduct of a bodhisattva, and do not depend on the 253 vows for that perfect conduct. The supreme sangha is composed of arhats, pratyekabuddhas, and bodhisattvas who have already attained the path of seeing.

When you take refuge in the sangha, the ultimate benefit is that in every lifetime you will meet the supreme teachers. Ultimately you will become enlightened. The temporary benefit is that you are protected from being misled. Additionally, the merit of being a respectable follower of the sangha will continuously result in a good human life. You will not fall into any one of the eight unfavorable lives (in a hell realm, hungry ghost realm, animal realm, savage realm, sleeping god realm[1], human but overwhelmed by wrong views, a realm where the buddhadharma does not exist, with disabilities that prevent one from practicing and understanding the dharma).

Therefore, if you reflect on the immense benefits, it is very important to begin by taking refuge. As the ground of Mind Training practice, taking refuge is essential. Ideally you should also study the ways to develop the

[1] In this case, the positive karma of having done lots of shamatha meditation leads to rebirth in a god realm, but, because of having a dull and confused mind, one simply sleeps there for thousands or even millions of years.

merit of your refuge vows and how to prevent mistakes that may spoil that precious merit.

After you have taken refuge you can take further vows. Whether you take a lay-person's vows, novice vows, Brahmacharya vows (completely free from family life, living like Milarepa), or full monk's vows will be in accordance with your capacity for renouncing samsara. Finally, after that you can receive the bodhisattva vow. Without refuge vows you cannot receive the layperson's or monastic vows, and without those vows you have no ground for taking the bodhisattva vow. Without the bodhisattva vow, there is no basis from which to practice lojong.

Ordinary Shiné

Another aspect of the preliminaries is recognizing that the mind needs to be tamed. Thoughts should be controlled. In order to accomplish this you need to learn shiné or calm abiding meditation. *Shi* is short for the Tibetan word *shiwa* which means "tranquil", "calm", or "peaceful". *Né* is short for *népa* which means to "rest" or "abide". There are many kinds of shiné practice, but the initial level of shiné is crucial to learn in order to have strong stability of concentration. In order to learn that concentration meditation, you first need to know how to sit.

Sitting Posture

1. You must sit up straight when you meditate. Your legs can be fully crossed in the full lotus position, or alternatively they can be half-crossed with the right leg out and the left in. Generally, a person with longer legs sits on a higher cushion, but how high your seat is really depends on your physical proportions. It is important that your spine be completely straight. Your stomach is slightly drawn inward and back, while your abdomen is very slightly resting forward for balance. This keeps the central part of the body very straight and it is the ideal posture for meditation.

2. To enhance a straight central torso, your shoulders should also be balanced and straight.

3. As for your hands, you can place them together in the posture of meditation. This means the palms of the hands face up, right hand on top of the left in your lap. Raise your shoulders slightly up and backward, such that the lengths of the arms are gently pressed against the sides of your body. This position further reinforces an upright and straight spine. Alternatively, you can rest your hands palms down on your knees, taking care to keep the shoulders straight.

4. Your neck should be slightly curved so that your chin is slightly tucked in towards your chest.

5. Your eyes are half open, looking ahead and cast slightly downward.

6. Your mouth should neither be open nor pressed firmly closed. Your lips should be relaxed in a very natural position.

7. Breathing is mainly through the nose and not the mouth.

These are the essential points of a correct physical posture for meditation. Now for instructions on how the mind should concentrate.

In order to train the mind to concentrate, you must focus on your breath. There are a number of techniques to accomplish this. First, picture your breath as a very narrow, bright beam of light. As you inhale and exhale you concentrate on this straight beam of light entering and exiting your nostrils. As it enters your nostrils it flows up through your nose and curves down through your body, all the way to the level of your navel then back out again.[1] Count each breath—that is one exhalation and one inhalation—until you reach twenty-one breaths in total. You can start with a gentle inhalation, then start counting from sending out and taking in your breath—one. Out and in—two. Out and in—three, and so forth. Breathe

[1] Some may find it strange to visualize the breath moving all the way down to the navel. You may alternatively picture it flowing down into your lungs instead.

in a relaxed way, pausing after each inhalation and exhalation. In order to help with the counting you can use
a mala (meditation beads) or a hand held counter. Count
twenty-one breaths and then take a short break. Then
start again, counting your breaths up to twenty-one, all
the while picturing your breath as a beam of light. When
you first try to do this, your mind may be distracted and
it will be hard to count twenty-one breaths. Do not be
concerned, even if it is very difficult at first. Just keep
calmly placing your concentration back on your breath.
Counting twenty-one breaths with good concentration
will develop tranquility in your body, speech and mind.
When you can manage to count twenty-one breaths
without any disturbance or distraction you will already
have achieved a very good quality concentration. When
you can count twenty-one breaths many times with the
same quality of concentration, your mind will be quickly
habituated to this discipline.

When you can count twenty-one breaths enough times
that the total number of breaths is twenty-one thousand,
you will have really achieved a good result: true tranquility. Obviously, this takes time. Counting twenty-one
breaths can be done in approximately five minutes. This
means that each hour you can count up to approximately
two-hundred and fifty-two breaths. To complete the full
twenty-one thousand breaths would take around three
and one-half days of continuous concentration. Of course

you can take breaks in between! For example, if you concentrate for eight hours each day, for ten and one-half
days, you would also be able to accomplish twenty-one
thousand breaths. If you can accomplish this, the results
will be excellent.[1]

At this point it is also good to apply some analytical
philosophy. As you concentrate your mind on the breath,
consider the relationship of mind and breath. Is the mind
the same as the breath? Is the mind different from the
breath? At first we understand that mind is not the same
as the breath; the breath is something for the mind to
focus on so it is not the same as the mind. At the same
time, a mind that is focused on the image of the breath
is *not separate* from the breath. This is because in order
to have a vision of the breath to focus on, the mind and
the breath also cannot be entirely separate. In fact, neither
one can exist independently. Without the mind, this type
of focused breathing isn't possible. *Breathe out, breathe in.*
Does that exist on its own? No, because it is controlled.
Without the focus of mind, you will not breathe like that.
The mind and the breath depend on each other to "exist"
as we experience them. As is the case with all phenomena,
things that are perceived and the mind that perceives are

[1]If at first counting is too difficult, you may simply keep track of time
instead: every five minutes equals twenty-one breaths. Concentrate for five
minutes, then take a short break.

the same. So the mind and the breath are neither of the same nature nor different either. This is the nature of illusion. It is empty, like a dream. Allow yourself to experience the mind and the breath as neither separate nor one. With this understanding, you should not cling to either mind or breath as truly existent while you are meditating.

More Shiné Practices

Once you have achieved the very stable shiné described above, you can use it for all kinds of things. There are in fact many different shiné practices so you can apply your skill in concentration to control and subdue many different distractions.

If you want to eventually control the many subtle distractions that afflict everyone, which is in fact the only way to cultivate persistent diligence for meditation, you must *first* control the major distractions that occur on the very surface of our experience. On the surface level, the many temporary pleasures of life provide no shortage of possible distractions, and in order to eventually achieve the goal of controlling the very subtle distractions you must begin by controlling these surface-level ones. What follows is a specific series of shiné practices designed to enable to you control those distractions. They have specific purposes, and after they are mastered you do not need to continue to practice them.

Remedy for Desire:
Concentration on the repulsiveness of the body

The most effective way to remedy the power of desire is to concentrate on the impermanence of the body. First visualize your body as clearly as you can. Try to really understand and know that it is a collection of parts that all depend on each other—the skeleton is a collection of bones joined by ligaments, it contains and protects many organs, it is covered by a network of muscles, there is flesh, fat, the circulatory system, the nervous system, etc. and wrapped around it like a bag is your skin. Now picture a spot of decay the size of the tip of your thumb on your forehead, between your eyes. That spot right there is rotting. What colour is it? What colors will it become? Think of the progression of putrid colors a rotting corpse goes through. Now those colors are progressing on your own forehead. Then the decay starts to spread all over your body. Your whole body is rotting, putrifying, and actually starts falling apart. Your rotten flesh falls in pieces to the floor all around you. Your organs also rot, decay, and fall to pieces on the floor. Now only your skeleton is left whole, together with one tiny piece of fresh flesh on the top of each foot, close to your big toes. Those two tiny spots, each the size of the tip of your thumb, are all that remain untouched by decay. Now even your skeleton starts to disintegrate, falling in scattered pieces on the floor. That heap of bones that made up your skeleton now starts to expand and grow. It grows vastly, until it is almost inconceivably big. Wherever you live, whatever continent, picture your skeleton expanding to the very shores of the oceans on every side. East to West, North to South. Your bones are huge, a giant skull, giant spine, etc. Then slowly, ever so slowly, it begins to recondense and reconstitute, slowly returning to its former size, slowly reforming itself back into your seated position. Then when your skeleton is completely back to its familiar state, those tiny pieces of fresh flesh close to your toes begin to spread. From these, everything regrows: your organs, muscles, flesh and blood. In the end your face grows back. It all returns except for one small mark between your eyes, ready to decay again. Take a small break at this point, then begin the meditation again. After you have done this many times you will reach a point where your reaction towards your own body and the bodies of others is one of nausea and revulsion. When you have reached that point it is time to stop. When you have finished your meditation session, do not continue to picture that spot of decay there. As explained above, you must not cling to this as real in post-meditation.

Remedy for Anger:
Concentration on compassion and loving-kindness

The most effective way to remedy anger is to cultivate

loving-kindness and compassion. In order to cultivate compassion, you must concentrate on the suffering that permeates the minds of all sentient beings. There are three types of suffering that exist in the minds of all sentient beings: suffering, sadness, and disappointment. Suffering mind is the mind that is constantly suffering from one thing or another. This can be caused by physical pain, for example. A sad mind is principally caused by thinking in a particular way: what you needed did not happen, what you did not need happened, etc. Anything that contributes to sadness and depression is part of the sad mind. Unlike suffering and sadness that come from the inside, disappointment comes from the outside. Whoever and whatever hurts you or harms you, disappoints you. That is disappointment.

First think about these three kinds of suffering that afflict the mind. Now think about how others suffer from these three types of suffering. First concentrate on the tiniest creatures—ants, earthworms, etc. Think about how each and every individual ant has a mind, and how every mind, no matter how small, is afflicted by these three kinds of suffering. Try to really feel how they feel their suffering. Now gradually consider bigger and bigger sentient beings: dogs, cows, etc. concentrating on how each living creature has a mind, that mind is afflicted by three kinds of suffering, and try to feel their pain. This continues up until you consider the minds of humans. Feeling how others feel this constant pain, just like you, you can really experience their pain. Feeling their pain as strongly as your own, you now cultivate the wish that all sentient beings should be free from these three types of suffering.

Now consider the nature of this suffering, what is it? Where does it come from? Think about where suffering occurs: in the mind. Suffering permeates every moment of mind, every moment of mind carries sadness, disappointment, and subtle suffering. This is the real truth of the first noble truth: *there is suffering.* The mind never has a moment of peace. Now consider how if there is no suffering in an individual's mind, there is in fact no suffering at all. So what is mind? Investigate it closely and you will see that every moment of mind is impermanent, not solid or lasting. Moment to moment it changes, without a single, solid essence underlying it. Through this sincere investigation, you will discover that mind is in fact empty, that underlying it there is no such thing as a self. So in fact it is the mistaken belief in a self, the mistaken belief in the permanence of the mind, that underlies the experience of each of these three kinds of suffering. Now with the understanding that all beings—including yourself—suffer equally, and with the understanding that there is no self to suffer, that mind is empty, raise up the intense desire that all beings be freed from their suffering. Wishing that they be free from suffering is compassion. After you have generated the sincere wish that all beings be free from suffering, cultivate an equally intense wish for all sentient beings to experience happiness. Do this by calling to mind the fact that each living being has the same desire for happiness as you do, and then concentrate on generating the profound wish that every single sentient being experience true joy. That is loving-kindness.

This concentration is limitlessly meritorious. It produces limitless merit. This meditation is something you can practice for weeks, until you can comfortably and smoothly concentrate the moment you sit down for meditation: all beings suffer exactly as I do; suffering is in the mind; each moment of mind does not exist; the mind-stream is therefore empty and there is nothing to cling to; may all beings realize this and be free from suffering. All beings wish for happiness exactly as I do; may all beings experience true joy.

Remedy for Pride: Where am I?

The next concentration is the ideal remedy for pride and self-clinging. This meditation allows us to understand that there is no self to cling to and be proud of.

Begin by considering the nature of clinging or attachment. Is clinging independent? No, it cannot be independent, because it requires that there is something to be attached to. For example, "that is *my* phone" or "those are *my* shoes." Now think about the way you cling to yourself as special, unique, the center of your own world. What are you clinging to? What is it about *you* that *you* are attached to? To your form? Consider the different things that make up your form. Think about just your skin, from the tips of your toes to the top of your head, from back to front, just the skin. Ask yourself: "is *that* me?" Then think about your flesh, the muscle, fat, organs, etc. everywhere. Take the time to look in biology books to get an impression of flesh, then really use your mind to picture your *own* flesh. Where is "me"? Is *that* me? Am *I* in any part of my flesh? In my heart? In my head? Now think about your veins. Mentally strip away the flesh and muscles and organs in your body and think about your whole circulatory system. Where am *I* in that network of veins, arteries, capillaries? There is certainly still a feeling of self as you do this, as you look for yourself, but try to locate it somewhere. You will find that there is no "me" anywhere.

Now think about all the liquid in your body: blood, lymph, water, urine, etc. Is there anything there in all those liters of various liquids that is *you*? Now think about your bones. Concentrate on every part of yourself, thinking about the bones in every part of your body. Slowly consider each and every part of your bone structure. Look for something to cling to as a self there: is *that* me? Now examine the space in your body: there is space in your intestines, space in the marrow of your bones, space in your veins, in your lungs, ears, etc. Can you find a self anywhere there?

Then think about all the elements in your body, the air, the heat, the cool. Is *that* me? Now think about the sense consciousnesses, the distinct capacity for awareness of each sense organ, and try to find a self there. Is my *self* in my consciousness of sound? If you cling to a self in your consciousness of sound, how does the consciousness of seeing occur? Where am *I* in seeing? What about tasting, touching, smelling, or even thinking? How can the self be there separately in each of these senses? If each sense consciousness has one self, you have at least five or six selves—you are not one, you are many. That would mean that for each sense consciousness there is a separate self. How can you be many selves? If you think that you have one self altogether for all of these, then it should follow that you can hear with your eyes, see with your skin, etc. If you cannot find a self in any of those parts, then collectively where could it possibly be? That is how you meditate.

Then in post-meditation, consider how your idea of "self" is just an illusion. You have examined each and every part of your body and did not find a self there. It's just an illusion. Therefore, since there is nothing to think of as your self, there is nothing to cling to. This will reduce the clinging you have to your*self.* It will reduce pride and ego.[1] I recommend working on this concentration for about one week.

---

[1]Shiné for subduing pride is the implementation of the practice of lojong. For that reason I did not mention the Preliminary Practices known in Tibetan as Ngöndro here.

Remedy for Ignorance:
The links of interdependence

In this meditation you are removing the basic ignorance regarding the real existence of self and others. Traditionally, in working on this meditation Buddhists consider the entire set of twelve interdependent links that bring about Samsaric existence, beginning with basic ignorance and ending with death. In brief, the twelve links are: 1. ignorance; 2. habitual tendencies; 3. consciousness; 4. name and form; 5. the six bases of sensory experience; 6. contact; 7. feeling; 8. craving; 9. grasping; 10. becoming; 11. birth; 12. old age and death. In this case, however, do this meditation as I describe it below, applying this analytical process to the various links without counting through the twelve in a forced way.

Begin by thinking about how your life started. Think about that very first moment when your parents conceived you. That is the very first moment of *you*. Is that, therefore, the truth of your existence? If so, then ask yourself if your life, your body, came from your mother *or* your father. If it came from your father, why did you need a mother? If it came from your mother, why did you need a father? If it came from one or the other, it must have come exactly as it is now, having preexisted "you" in some way. At the same time, if it was not in either your father or your mother, how could it be from them together? Leaving that aside for a moment, think about that *you* at the moment of conception. Was it really you? Were you attached to yourself then? If there is no self-clinging, then how is it you? Now think about this: if you came from your mother or your father, and if you have self-clinging, then that self-clinging must be to your father or to your mother. Where are *you*? Since independently existing self-clinging is impossible, and your body without your self-clinging isn't you, which came first, the body or the self-clinging? Independently, neither can exist. This is the examination of form. Now think about your feelings. Where, at this moment, do feelings exist? Are feelings in self-clinging, or in the body? If they are in the body, then even without self-clinging, without a sense of self, you must have feelings. If they exist only in self-clinging, then even without a body you must have had feelings. This is the examination of feelings.

Now think about the growth of life. Does growth exist in the mind? Or is it in the physical form which has no mind? If growth is in flesh, bone, etc. then without mind, a body has to grow as a life. If it is only in the mind, then life has to grow even without form. Therefore, life does not exist independently either in flesh and bone, or in the self-clinging mind. If neither can be said to independently have "growth" or "life", then how can putting them together make it? The beginning of life is a mirage; the growth of life is a mirage. Now consider life itself. If life exists, does it exist at the start or in the growth? If it existed at the start, then you did not need to grow because life was already there. But if life exists in growth, then you can't have a beginning. What is it? Where is it? In its beginning, in growth, in aging, in death? If life is in death, how can death be death? In that case it would be life. But without life, how can death come? Where is death? What is death? Death must also be a mirage. Does death exist in death, or in life?

Now expand your range and apply this reasoning to every part of yourself. Does any of it exist independently? Even your consciousness? Try to figure out if any of your many sensitive thoughts are in the body or in the mind. For instance, consider the thought of clinging to your own beauty. If that attachment to your beauty exists in your mind, then even without a body you will cling to your own beauty. And without a form, where is the beauty to cling to? If, on the other hand, that clinging exists in the flesh, bones and skin, then even without a mind the physical form must experience that clinging. Apply this reasoning to each and every thought, and before long you will discover it is all mirages. Self, other, form, feelings, everything. It is there when all the factors—mind, body and experience—are together, but it is definitely not there as an independent reality. Therefore, everything is a dream-like illusion. This meditation will develop a precise understanding of the interdependent nature of phenomena. In Tibetan we call this *chöki shérap*. It is the perfect remedy to ignorance.

Final thoughts on the preliminaries

To conclude this section on the preliminaries here is a short review. As practice that is preliminary to lojong itself, shiné is indispensable. The meditations above will help you to subdue the five mental poisons and all agitation in the mind. It is important to start with the first one, counting the breath, and to develop your concentration with that. This is because once you are really proficient at that practice, the other ones can easily be practiced well. So to summarize the shiné practices:

1. Shiné of counting the breaths: remedy for constant thoughts and agitation.

2. Shiné of decomposing your body: remedy for physical desire and distractions.

3. Shiné of cultivating loving-kindness and compassion: remedy for anger and jealousy.

4. Shiné of searching for the self: remedy for ego and pride.

5. Shiné of concentration on interdependence: remedy for ignorance.

In order to maintain a good quality of meditation while

you are concentrating on all these points, there are a few things to keep in mind and to put into practice. First of all, if you start to feel agitated, take a moment to relax. If you feel drowsy, discipline your body. Review the points of correct meditation posture and sit up straight. This will push your energy back up to your mind. Be vigilant with respect to your awareness throughout your meditation. Be constantly mindful of when to relax, when to focus, things like that. It will also be helpful if you have good eating habits. Basically this means not eating too much. Ideally, when you eat your stomach should be only half-filled with food, ¼ filled with liquid, and ¼ empty. If you are in strict retreat, do not eat after 1pm until the following morning. That is really the best for concentration, although it is clearly not possible for people who are working. Drinking tea, green tea or black tea, is fine. Coffee, however, is not good for meditation because after a jolt of energy you will become drowsy. If you are in strict retreat, you can wake up around 5 am and do meditation until 10pm and then sleep after that. Before 10pm is too early to sleep. People who are working and not in retreat must of course adjust their time according to their schedules.

If you have the opportunity to do a shiné retreat, the best would be to begin by accomplishing the concentration on breathing such that you can count twenty-one thousand breaths. Each of the other four practices can be done for three weeks each. The great master Shantideva explains that the meditation of superior view (*lhaktong* or *vipashyana*) can destroy all the defilements *only* from the basis of stable shiné:

> *Understanding that the meditation*
> *of superior view that has fully incorporated shiné*
> *will vanquish all the defilements,*
> *first you must seek shiné,*
> *and that is accomplished by delighting in freedom*
> *from worldly desires.*
> Bodhicaryavatara, ch. 8, verse 4

There is one final shiné meditation to share here. It is the auspicious shiné of concentrating on the Buddha. Visualize as clearly as you can the figure of a Buddha sitting in front of you. He is seated on the most precious seat you can imagine, and behind him is a magnificent *bodhi* tree. His body is golden and radiant, and he is looking directly at you with boundless love and compassion. Concentrate carefully on each part of the Buddha: his beautiful gaze, his eyes, his mouth, his hair, his chest, shoulders, arms and legs, posture. Concentrate on him and generate intense devotion for him. When you have raised up this great devotion, the Buddha turns into light and dissolves into you. There are many benefits from this concentration. In the short term, it is beneficial because it further trains your concentration and causes you to directly focus on the Buddha. Another short-term benefit is that it trains the imprint in your mind that your meditation will be guided by your own wisdom. Ultimately, the benefit is that you will finally develop into a full Buddha and benefit limitless beings limitlessly.

Shakyamuni Buddha

THE SECOND POINT

Train in the Two Bodhicittas

The Second Point: Key instructions for training in the two bodhicittas, beginning with ultimate bodhicitta.

The actual practice of Mind Training develops bodhicitta, the altruistic intention, which has two aspects: relative and ultimate. While the practice of relative bodhicitta is very effective for accumulating merit, training in ultimate bodhicitta develops your wisdom. Mind Training therefore combines the two accumulations of merit and wisdom that complement and support one another.

Although it may seem counterintuitive to begin with ultimate bodhicitta, it is necessary in order to develop conventional bodhicitta correctly. This is because without being grounded in the wisdom of emptiness, it is easy to reify the methods employed in the cultivation of conventional bodhicitta. If you take self, other and what passes between them as real, even the practice of generating loving-kindness can become a cause for suffering and worry. Therefore we begin with ultimate bodhicitta.

Ultimate bodhicitta is wisdom, a perfect understanding of the true nature of mind and of phenomena. There are two stages to developing ultimate bodhicitta, the first of which is to acquire an analytical understanding of emptiness. Later, through the meditation of superior view you will have a direct experience of the empty nature of all phenomena.

Analyze the unborn nature of mind.

While learning the tools to apply analytical meditation to outer objects is useful to understand their emptiness, the most important point is to directly experience the nature of mind. Because it cannot be realized through analytical meditation alone and requires direct experience, it is also the most challenging thing to understand.

Analytical meditation can, however, be used to *approach* the nature of mind. This can be most easily done by someone who is experienced in shiné meditation and has achieved a very stable mind. To begin with, you have already analyzed objects, forms, experiences, everything, and confirmed that it is nothing other than the mind that experiences it. Now consider this: if there is no mind, then shapes, colors, forms, sounds, smells, tastes, sensations and feelings *cannot exist*. Where there is no mind, there is no*thing*. Nothing can exist on its own, without mind. Sounds are not harmonious or discordant, tastes are not sweet or bitter, forms are not beautiful or repulsive. Further, without functioning sense conscious-nesses, there are no phenomena. Sound, for example, does not exist on its own. Without an ear consciousness to hear it, there is no sound. Everything that we perceive and experience is nothing more or less than habitual patterns in the mind ripening exactly as though in a dream. All this can be confirmed with analytical meditation and the meditation of resting in mind's nature. We will therefore begin with analytical meditation.

Try to understand the nature of your mind objectively as it passes through time. You will find that it is impossi-ble to locate. First of all, the past no longer exists so there is no mind there. The future has yet to arise, so it is not to be found there either. There is only the present moment, and that changes continually. Mind itself is momentary, arising as a series of moments that each cease as the next arises. Mind is in fact a continuum of moments. Analyze every moment: how does it exist? Where in this moment are the forms you see, the sounds you hear, the smells you smell, the tastes you taste, the sensations you feel? At this moment do you experience happiness, suffering, or neutral feelings? Where are those feelings, are they located in the mind or in the objects? Where is the mind, and where is the object? Think about your favorite song. Where is the song—in the radio? In your ear? In your

mind? *Where* does that song occur? If the song is really
there outside of you, what need is there for your mind?
If it is really there in your mind, then why do you need
the song? Look for it in your mind: is it there in each
moment of mind? Does the whole song arise from and
belong to each individual moment of mind? How does
it arise there, remain there, vanish from there? If you
can't find it there, if it is not in a single moment of mind,
how could it be there in the continuum as a whole? Now
analyze the joy you experience listening to that song, cultivate that feeling of joy. Where is it? Is it in the song? Or
is it in your mind? It doesn't make sense to say that joy is
in a song, since that would mean your experiencing mind
doesn't need to be there for that joy to occur. If that was
the case, an insect hearing the same song would experience the same joy as you. It also does not make sense to
say the joy is in your mind independent of the song, otherwise why is the joy linked to that song? If that was the
case, you could experience the joy of the song without the
song altogether. Clearly, the joy does not exist in either
the song or the mind. If feelings of happiness and suffering are there in each moment of mind, then there is no
need for forms, smells, sounds, etc. If it is in the mind,
the mind *has* it and requires nothing else.

Generate a feeling of sadness and analyze it the same
way. Where does it come from? How does it arise, persist,
and disappear? You can also experiment with a gentle

sensation of pain. Using a small needle, gently prick yourself without fully puncturing the skin. Analyze the feeling that arises. Where does it arise? In the needle? In your skin? In your mind? You will discover that this process is one in which you are continually analyzing your own mind. This is called mindfulness.

When you apply this analytical mindfulness to objects you will freshly experience not only the objects, but the very nature of mind as unborn, not remaining, unceasing. It is neither one nor many. It is free of labeling and appearances. You will realize that mind is naturally empty, and when you experience that emptiness you will also understand that even emptiness is not there in the mind. It is beyond conceptualization. When you reach this stage through analysis, just rest in the resulting experience. Without imagining any shape, color, anything at all, just effortlessly observe the experience of mind. When a thought arises, examine its nature simultaneous with its arising. You do not need to have hopes or doubts about it, you do not need to accept or reject it, you do not need to follow that thought anywhere. Analyze it directly and let it subside, just like that. Like a piece of paper that has been rolled up, you may unroll it but it will spring back to its shape naturally and effortlessly. Doing this, you will have the stable experience of the nature of mind as neither existing nor not existing. There is nothing to label or identify, because it has always been there. Du-

alistic mind is finished. Unborn mind is the nature of
your mind, it is the nature of mind of all sentient beings,
and equally the nature of mind of Buddhas. Just as the
space filling a valley is not separate from the space filling the sky, the unborn nature of mind is one. It has no
locus, no origin, and no basis. It is unborn, like cosmic
space. And much like space, if you look into the vastness
of mind there is *nothing* to see. Once you have caught
that glimpse of mind as a knowing continuum, you can
put aside the analytical meditation and rest your mind
directly on this understanding.

Our current experience of mind is veiled by ignorance,
but happily that ignorance is not intrinsic to it, ignorance
is not its nature. Rather, wisdom is its innate quality. If
the mind was fundamentally ignorant, freedom from
that ignorance would be impossible. As it is, even that ignorant mind, when put to work trying to reflect on itself,
will conclude that there is in fact *nothing* to seize upon as
existent. When that occurs, basic ignorance will dissolve
naturally and spontaneously. That is awakening. Just as
clouds in the sky appear and disappear without having to
be gathered and stored somewhere, and just as they never
change the intrinsically clear nature of the sky, so ignorance need not be consciously gathered and removed and
even when present does not affect the nature of mind.
Another useful example is darkness. What is darkness?
It is actually completely without substance, it is the mere

experience of light not reaching the eye. Light appears to dispel darkness, but in fact there is nothing to dispel. The innate wisdom of mind causes ignorance to disappear just as naturally as light allows one to see.

Purify the strongest negative emotion first.

Negative emotions are not our friends. For that reason, although the analogy I will use here is somewhat disturbing it does get to the heart of the matter. To quickly defeat an enemy army with as little fighting as possible, the best strategy is to identify the strongest fighter and knock him (or her) out first. Likewise, most people have one negative emotion that is stronger than all the others. If you can begin by purifying that one first, the others will lose their power and retreat with relatively little struggle. To undermine the power of the negative emotions you first need to understand them. To understand something properly it must be observed. The best way to observe a powerful negative emotion is in the controlled laboratory of your own calmly abiding, thought-free mind. We can use anger as an example. While meditating, after resting the mind one-pointedly in clarity and emptiness for some time, work yourself into a terrible rage. The stronger the emotion, the stronger the contrast, the more there is to observe, and the better it will work as practice. From a deeply restful state it may be quite dif-

ficult to conjure up such a strong negative emotion, but
you can use your imagination to think up an offensive,
angering situation; or draw on your memories—think
back to some moment when you were deeply offended,
hurt, or attacked. Once it has been aroused you should,
as objectively as possible, analytically contemplate its nature and its attributes. Where did it come from? Does it
have a shape? Location? Does it have any substance? You
will uncover its illusory qualities and it will dissipate by
itself. When it dissipates the mind is once again resting
in its naturally pure state. You can apply this practice to
desire, jealousy, or any other disturbing emotion. Arouse,
study, neutralize. By developing this habit and ability
you will with more and more ease analyze the nature
of whatever arises in the mind. As you understand that,
whatever arises there will disappear by itself.

Over time you will also begin to clearly perceive that
the variety of disturbing emotions is limited. In the
abhidharma teachings, there are said to be a total of thirty
disturbing emotions. These are divided into ten root disturbing emotions and twenty secondary ones. Every single
disturbing emotion that you experience, when analyzed
thoroughly and carefully, will be found to be one or a com-
bination of these. The ten root or fundamental disturbing
emotions are: ignorance (with respect to the teachings of
the Buddha); attachment; anger; arrogance; doubt (with
respect to the Four Noble Truths); belief in a self beyond or

within the five aggregates; extreme views regarding the
self or aggregates (that they are either permanent or nihil-
istically disconnected from everything); perverted beliefs
(believing that what is true is not true); holding onto the
superiority of those three beliefs listed above; and finally
belief that misguided discipline or ascetic practices will
liberate you. The twenty secondary disturbing emotions
are permutations of the root disturbing emotions. According to the commentary of Mipham Rinpoche, the great
19th century Lama and scholar, seven can be said to belong
to the category of the three poisons of ignorance, anger,
and attachment. These include: hypocrisy, lack of con-
science, shamelessness, heedlessness, forgetfulness, inat-
tention, and distraction. Two belong to the two categories
of ignorance and attachment: pretense and concealment.
Lack of faith and lethargy are two that belong to the category of ignorance. Five belong to the category of anger:
fury, resentment, spite, hostility, and envy. Finally, four
belong to the category of attachment: stinginess, self-in-
fatuation, laziness and excitement. This describes the full
range of possible unwholesome mental states.

As your practice of this meditation matures, applying
the remedy to emotions will happen automatically. You
can picture it like this: if you are watching a blacksmith
shaping heated steel, as he strikes the steel sparks will
fly. Some last long enough to keep burning for a short
time, some will disappear before they even touch the

ground. Those sparks are like your emotions. You must train your mind so that even when the "sparks" of your emotions arise, they will simply disappear before they contact the ground.

Even the remedy naturally liberates itself.

In the end, even the remedy does not exist. Where there is no poison, what need is there for an antidote?

We can use fire as an analogy. To make a fire, you can rub two pieces of wood together. Once the flame is ignited, the wood is consumed. When the wood is consumed, the fire also disappears. The two pieces of wood are the experiencer—the mind—and the object experienced, also the mind. The dualistic approach of the experiencer, the meditator, searching for his or her mind, is akin to rubbing two sticks together. The realization of the emptiness of both, when it occurs, blazes like a fire and consumes both subject and object. Therefore blazing wisdom that is insight into emptiness, the remedy, naturally dissipates when its fuel—the dualistic separation between subject and object—is consumed.

What this means is that once the true nature of phenomena is understood, the perceiving mind that analyzes will dissolve by itself. Because the perceiving mind cannot exist independently of objects to perceive, without objects to cause it to arise, the perceiving mind naturally

ceases. Mind is no longer trapped in the duality of perceiver and perceived. Mind stops running after the objects of the six senses, whether forms, sounds, smells, or
thoughts, etc. Ignorance is cleared away and the remedy
against ignorance then naturally ceases.

Now this is not to say that all experience ceases after
the wisdom of emptiness burns it up. It's not the case
that there are suddenly no more objects in the world.
The difference is that what mind experiences as objects
while under the control of duality will be radically transformed. When mind is freed of duality, the senses are
likewise freed, and it follows that the experience of objects is free from duality. That is the experience of the
liberated mind.

Rest in the essence of mind,
the basis of everything.

When the perceiving mind, its object (the perceived),
and the remedy all disappear, your mind is no longer
engaged with duality. Free of concepts, it is boundless.
You can simply meditate. Rest with this unobstructed,
unborn mind.

At first, it must of course be maintained with con-
scious vigilance. It will happen that a thought will flash
suddenly across your mind, then another, and another...
this will interrupt the meditative state. At this point,

rather than focusing on the thoughts as disruptive, study their innate nature. When their empty nature is recognized, mind will return naturally and spontaneously to its restful state. This process will become effortless, and eventually every passing thought will blend seamlessly into the unborn nature of mind as soon as it arises. In this profound non-dualistic state, each thought, instead of being experienced as an interruption or distraction, will be experienced as a spontaneous manifestation of innate wisdom.

Unborn mind is in fact the basis of everything. After experiencing it, your meditation practice will then change into resting in the direct experience of mind. By this meditation, you will develop ultimate bodhicitta, the wisdom of mind itself.

In post meditation, know that all phenomena are illusory.

During meditation, one experiences the unborn nature of mind. In the post-meditation state, an advanced meditator should experience the manifestations of mind—all phenomena—as illusory.

A useful and often-used metaphor for this way of experiencing phenomena is a magic show. During a magic show, a magician can cause his or her audience to see and experience many things as real that are nothing but optical illusions. A magician may use all kinds of devices to cause a tiger to appear. For the audience, there is a tiger. It can produce fear, wonder, even attachment. But the magician sees the tiger as a product of the ropes, mirrors, wood, etc. that he or she has used to create the illusion. That magician will still see the tiger, but the difference between the magician's experience of the tiger and the audience's experience of the tiger is that the magician will not, even for one moment, believe the tiger really exists. While there is obviously a big difference between a realized meditator and a great magician, it provides a useful parallel. The meditator, like the magician, has the same sense perceptions as the rest of us, but experiences phenomena differently. This is because the realized meditator understands the illusory nature of everything that arises, as intimately and surely as the magician knows the illusory nature of a magic trick.

Abandon all hope for results.

Meditation must not be undertaken with the expectation of experiencing results. When results are experienced, they must not become objects of attachment. If meditation practice is goal-driven, or if results become an object of attachment, the practice itself will be spoiled. Your meditation will be one more bad habit, and not produce the lasting result of insight into the empty nature of mind and phenomena.

For meditation to be effective, it must not be undertaken with worries about whether one is qualified, will experience results, or if the practice is worthwhile. Similarly, one must not have expectations about realization, results, and experiences. For meditation to be effective, the mind placed in meditation must be uncontrived.

One should also not grasp at the results of meditation. Many things can arise, positive and negative. One may experience sickness or bliss, suffering or clarity, powerful good dreams, powerful bad dreams, or no dreams at all. The point is, to seek out results or be attached to whatever you believe are the results of your practice is compulsive, deluded behavior. It is critical to abandon your expectations in order to allow the practice to work.

Second, the instructions on training in the union of
the conventional and ultimate bodhicitta:
Practice alternately the two, giving and taking.

Tonglen, giving and taking, is truly the principal practice of Mind Training. "Giving and taking" refers to giving all your merit, happiness and contentment to others, and taking their suffering onto yourself. This very profound practice combines the practice of relative bodhicitta with the view of ultimate bodhicitta. Clearly, you will not physically find yourself suffering from every disease known to humankind by practicing this meditation, or experience the heartbreak, anger, or other suffering of others explicitly. It is important to begin with cultivating the view of ultimate bodhicitta in order to not experience this too materialistically.

First you must engender the correct view, cultivated in the previous practice. You must understand the nature of mind as unborn, of phenomena as empty. You must understand that everything is like a mirage. Now think about all sentient beings, how they suffer physically and mentally because of the illusions they take to be real. For as long they labor under the illusion of self as real and suffering as real, sentient beings can truly benefit from your compassion, even while you know it is empty. Therefore raise up powerful compassion and love towards all sentient beings. While that compassion and love will be experienced by others simply as compassion and love, you must remember to apply the view of emptiness cultivated in the previous practice and understand that the nature of love and compassion is not separate from the unborn nature of mind.

Here, we can think back to three purified spheres of agent, action, and object mentioned at the very outset. In this case, you are the agent, compassion and love are the action, and all sentient beings are the object. All three are illusory, but for as long as the object—sentient beings— experience the world dualistically, they will nonetheless benefit from your compassionate action. For as long as a sentient being has self-clinging, according to their own illusion they have much benefit to gain and can be relieved of their suffering. Now you can help them by powerfully exerting your unemotional, unattached, unborn compassion. Basically, you understand the illusion and now you can manipulate it. Now you are the magician.

Compassion without attachment is the perfect cause. Knowing the nature of unborn mind, and knowing the illusions of sentient beings despite the fact that their minds are also unborn, you will bring about the perfect result. This is because for as long as sentient beings have self-clinging, they have the illusion of suffering. Therefore the opposite of suffering is equally true for them—they also can experience the illusion of getting help. For as long as they have the illusion that they can be harmed, they have the illusion that they can be helped, they can gain happiness from someone who is helpful. Now, on the basis of that illusion, you can be that helper. Grounded in genuine compassion and loving kindness, you should make wishes for the well-being of all sentient beings so that every single one without exception can receive your help.

The Practice of Tonglen

To put this into effect, use your breathing. Breathe out: *As much compassion and love as I have, as much merit as I have gained, and all good wishes, may it reach every sentient being without exception and bring them happiness.* Breathe in: *As much suffering as sentient beings have, may it all,*

without exception, come into me. Breathing out is like giving medicine; breathing in is like drawing the poison out
of a wound. Your breath spreads everywhere, like light.
It is illusory, like the sun's reflection. The sun is reflected
equally in every pond, puddle, and drop of water; the sun
appears and shines in all those places simultaneously. But
it isn't really there. Like that, all your compassion, love and
merit spreads out everywhere at once, and all the suffering
of every sentient being is removed.

The very basis of tonglen, therefore, is the union of
conventional and ultimate bodhicitta. Many other things
are also joined in this practice: the union of the two accumulations of merit and wisdom is accomplished, as
well as the union of skillful method and wisdom; and
the union of the form body (*rupakaya*: nirmanakaya
and sambhogakaya; the physical forms that living beings perceive as a Buddha) with the body of truth nature
(dharmakaya: the truth nature of awakened mind and
all phenomena) is accomplished. These three can be understood simply as ground, path and fruit. The ground is
the union of the conventional and ultimate bodhicitta;
the path is the two accumulations of merit and wisdom
as well as the union of method and wisdom; and the fruition, the result, is the two kayas, form and truth nature.

This practice, giving and taking, is like an incredible
shortcut. Everything is contained here. Traditionally, the
path of a bodhisattva, one who has engendered the altruistic intention of bodhicitta, is mapped out into five paths

and ten stages. The five paths are the path of accumulation, the path of preparation, the path of insight, the path of cultivation and the path of no more learning. It is at the level of the third path, the path of insight, that the aspiring practitioner attains the first stage, or *bhumi*. The ten stages and five paths converge at the end in full awakening. What is important to know here is that every aspect of the five paths, the ten stages, indeed your entire path to awakening, can be accomplished by this practice[1].

Place the two upon the breath.

This is the instruction for actual tonglen meditation: First you breathe in, taking in all the unbearable misery of living beings everywhere. As you inhale, you take in all their suffering, bad karma, and the root causes of all that misery. You thereby relieve all sentient beings of their suffering and the causes of suffering.

When you breathe out, think that you are giving all your good karma, happiness, and circumstances to sen-

[1] For it to be really effective you must practice tonglen as much as possible and in conjunction with cultivating the awareness of the unborn nature of mind. For a very dedicated meditator on retreat, I recommend alternating two hours of cultivating awareness of the unborn nature of mind with two hours of tonglen. Of course you may take a short break in between. This cycle can then be repeated once or twice more throughout the day: two hours of unborn nature, two hours of giving and taking. For those not on retreat, the proportionate time spent on each aspect should remain, though the time will of course be shorter.

tient beings everywhere. Imagine that all your good merit and conditions are absorbed by living beings.

In tonglen, we visualize the giving and taking in sync with the rhythm of our breathing out and in. During the meditation, mind follows the breath, out and in. It is like shiné meditation but with the focus on bodhicitta, the compassionate attitude of mind. The out-breath carries all your merit and happiness to them. The in-breath absorbs all their negative karma and suffering. Therefore, this meditation is aptly named giving and taking.

Once you are in the flow of giving and taking, you don't have to make yourself feel anything special. Simply focus on the altruistic bodhicitta attitude: take all suffering onto yourself, and give all your happiness to others. Breathe gently and do the giving and taking for as long as you can. It is good to do this training in many short intervals. Practice for a little while and then stop. Take a break and relax for a few moments. Then start again. In this way, you can do many short sessions with breaks in between. Don't worry if you find yourself distracted during the actual meditation. Simply be aware, and patiently place your focus back on the bodhicitta attitude.

It is important not to think that there is something physically being exchanged. Remember the view of ultimate bodhicitta. Thinking that something is too real can cause some trouble in your mind. It is therefore very important to regard everything as a mirage.

The Seven Points of Mind Training is, in essence, a

seven-point training in bodhicitta, the altruistic intention. The main goal is to develop bodhicitta while the mind is at the same time being trained to concentrate. Your mind will be pacified by shiné and all disturbances will fall away. Simultaneous with the pacification of your mind, bodhicitta will arise.

Three objects, three poisons, three roots of virtue.

In order to help sentient beings it is necessary to first understand their afflictions, the root causes of their afflictions, and then how to remedy them.

In general, we perceive the world in three ways. We could alternatively say that there are three categories of objects. Due to the ignorance in the minds of sentient beings, our perception of any object takes place in a heavy, unknowing state of mind. This characterizes the basic perception experienced by all sentient beings. Objects are thus perceived without any accurate or clear understanding. These objects may be referred to as unclear objects. Among unclear objects, some are deemed good or attractive to the perceiver, while others may be deemed bad or repulsive. Together, these three make up the three categories of objects perceived by sentient beings: unclear, attractive, and repulsive.

Accordingly, these three types of objects elicit emotional responses in us. We feel desire for that which we deem good; we feel aversion to that which we deem bad; and we are always in an unclear, unknowing state caused by the ignorance of the mind. Living beings experience very potent feelings of grasping at everything, as we have many desires. Even aversion is a form of grasping: if you reflect on it you will realize that aversion to something implies grasping at something else. The desires and aversions are so consuming that they create an experience of distaste in the mind. Equally unpleasant is the basic unclear state of mind that is ignorance.

Together, desire, aversion, and ignorance are the three poisons in the minds of all sentient beings. It is fitting to call them poisons because of the detrimental effects they have on the mind. They make us feel uneasy, dissatisfied, and unwell. Moreover, the three poisons arouse a great variety of negative emotions. When you act out of anger or jealousy, for example, you cause immediate suffering to everyone. You are also creating more causes of negative karma, more suffering for yourself and others.

Knowing that all living beings experience the three objects and the three poisons, we wish to cure them. In order to help them, we implement the Mind Training methods as an antidote to remove the poisons from our own mind as soon as they occur. When the poison of desire appears, recognize it as such and apply the concise method of lojong to counter it—to change it into a root of virtue:

*As I suffer this desire, may I take in the desires of all
sentient beings and relieve them. May all sentient beings
be released from all disturbing emotions caused by desire
and may all the resultant negative karma created by desire
mature on me rather than on others.*

Apply this same method of taking whenever aversion or ignorance appears. In this way, the three objects
and the three poisons become the three roots of virtue.
Grasping is transformed into non-grasping; aversion is
transformed into mental ease, or comfort; and ignorance
becomes the clarity of mind, neither downcast nor sleepy.
It is a mind imbued with fresh awareness.

In addition to taking in negativities, Mind Training
also trains you to give all virtues and good conditions
to others. Ultimately, you wish all sentient beings to be
enlightened. In this practice, you therefore wish to take
away the three poisons of a self-clinging mind and give
every sentient being non-grasping, comfort and clarity of
mind. You also wish that under these excellent conditions
innumerable virtues will take root, grow, and become perfected. Sentient beings will then accomplish the bodhisattva stages, and ultimately be liberated from samsara.

Train your conduct by means of the slogans.

In all your actions, train yourself in the points of Mind
Training. The root text is written in short slogans in

order to allow you to easily commit it to memory. You must remember the points and remind yourself of the meaning.

You should always try to engender the attitude of giving and taking. When things are going well for you, wish that all good conditions and results go to others. When you feel down and out, take on all the suffering of others and relieve them completely, right down to the tiniest experience of discomfort. You absorb them all into yourself through your own suffering.

Concluding remarks on Giving and Taking

The profundity of tonglen practice cannot be overestimated. By practicing it correctly and diligently, it is possible to attain the first bhumi in a single lifetime.

Convert Adversities into the Path of Awakening

The Third Point: Convert adversities into the path of awakening. Among ordinary and extraordinary instructions, begin with the first.

There are both ordinary and extraordinary instructions on converting adversities into the path of awakening. In this case, we first examine the ordinary instructions. These are then followed by three different extraordinary instructions.

When beings and the world are filled with evil, convert adversities into the path of awakening.

Due to their self-clinging and negative actions, living beings (and therefore the world) are filled with evil.

You should call to mind that suffering is the maturing and passing of bad karma. Like everything else, negative karma is also impermanent—it will eventually run itself out. Since the results of your own actions always ripen on you, it is better to deal with them now as best you can and be done with them.

The reason why the lojong methods are so special is that they show you how to take advantage of your negative karma. You can deploy the methods to actually transform every undesirable circumstance into an opportunity to practice the dharma.

How does this work? Your suffering connects you to the suffering of sentient beings by making you understand that suffering is universal. As you suffer, you can resolve to absorb all suffering. Your motivation, however, must be genuine. When it is, adverse conditions essentially become a means for you to accumulate good karma, or positive merit. Think: *I am suffering. Through my suffering, may I absorb all the suffering of others and relieve them.* This wish, grounded in relative bodhicitta, purifies your karma and, in effect, reduces your resistance to your own suffering.

> *Among the three extraordinary instructions,*
> *the first is how conventional bodhicitta is used*
> *to convert adversities into the path of awakening:*
> **Hold one fault accountable for all misfortunes.**

Whenever you suffer in negative circumstances or have conflicts with people, you should first know that it is the result of your own past negative actions. Bring to mind the slogan: *hold one fault accountable for all misfortunes.* That one fault is ego-clinging. It is the root cause of negativities. It is important to remember this truth. Finger pointing usually arouses more negative emotions and adds negative karma to your store, so don't waste time assigning blame to others or getting tangled in the never ending rounds of who's right. That only increases your suffering. By refraining from searching for an external cause for your suffering, you will feel less anxious about having to deal with the problems.

Since beginningless time, the minds of sentient beings have been engaged in samsaric activities. Uninterruptedly we have taken rebirths in both physical and mental forms. Despite the fact that the forms themselves are unreal, they have held our minds without pause. For these reasons, since beginningless time we have experienced the three kinds of suffering, to which you had a short introduction in the instructions on the shiné meditation to remedy anger.

Our current state of mind is not perfect. It is, in fact, a state of ignorance. What we are ignorant of is the true nature of our own mind so we mistakenly cling to the notion of a self, and a self-clinging mind is filled with suffering. That suffering, while very subtle, pervades a mind of ignorance. In many commentaries it is only vaguely explained as the subtle suffering that pervades everything. It has been mistakenly interpreted to mean that it pervades all objects—the cups and plates in your kitchen, for example, could be said to be pervaded with this subtle suffering. Based on my own investigation into how this form of suffering works I have drawn the conclusion that what is pervaded by subtle suffering is every moment of the mind-stream. Every moment of mind carries this suffering, and therefore every phenomenon perceived by it, every thought, every feeling is similarly pervaded by it. A mind that has not been tamed and that has not been pacified cannot experience even a single moment free from that pervasive suffering. This is particularly clear to those beings in the form and formless realms, highly accomplished in shiné meditation, who can accurately observe the suffering that thoroughly pervades the untamed and unpeaceful minds of beings in the desire realm—ourselves, for example. Then, of course, once you become a bodhisattva, you will see that the minds of all beings in the three realms are clearly untamed and not peaceful. In addition, as the great scholar Tsongkhapa observed, that suffering is the very basis for the experience of the other two forms of suffering. For after all, a mind that is tamed and peaceful is not laboring under the illusion that it is a self. So in a mind free of the pervasive, subtle suffering, who is there to suffer? Who is there to feel it? In the Tenjur, the sacred commentaries on the Buddhist scriptures, it is said that ordinary living beings do not recognize the suffering of subtle, pervading suffering. It is said that they feel it just as they would a hair lying in the palm of their hand. Bodhisattvas, on the other hand, are as acutely aware of that subtle pervading suffering as they would be of a strand of hair in their eye. One who can really perceive this is only a short step from fully understanding the other three points that together explain the profound meaning of the first noble truth as it is explained in the *Abhisamayalankara Prajnaparamita Upadesha shastra*: impermanence, no-self, and emptiness.

At the same time, we experience some happiness mixed with the suffering. This happiness is captivating and our mind gets attached to it even though it is impure. It does not last. In fact, it is ever changing. The moment we feel separated from the happiness we want, we suffer. In this way, the basic, subtle pervasive suffering unfailingly churns out additional suffering for us. That is the second kind of suffering.

In the meantime, in our relentless pursuit of happiness we act negatively, by either taking advantage of others or outright hurting them to get what we want. We create causes that will eventually and inevitably ripen into negative effects. When they do, we will experience rebirths in the realms of suffering. This is the third type of suffering.

Suffering is endless in the mind that clings to a self, because our selfish actions are endless. The one fault is therefore self-clinging.

Reflect on the great kindness of all beings.

If you can step away from self-clinging for a while, and try to reflect deeply, you will discover that there is another mind. This mind gives a fresh attitude, one that is diametrically opposed to self-centeredness. It is an open mind that replaces habitual self-concern with a genuine concern for the wellbeing of others. This mind of loving kindness is the very cause for you to break free of self-clinging mind.

A mind bent on benefiting others is a fertile field where virtues grow in abundance. Virtue, in any context, connotes an honest good free of any harm. Implicit in the meaning of "good" is usefulness and benefit to others. Kindness, generosity, and patience, for example, are universally recognized virtues that benefit others.

The reason we feel gratitude towards all sentient beings is that they provide us with never-ending opportunities to cultivate these virtues. Not only do we practice taking their suffering as our own, but in our daily encounters with them we are granted a precious chance to put our virtues into practice: when they behave in a self-centered way we can cultivate patience, kindness and generosity; and when they behave in a virtuous way we can cultivate sympathetic joy and make the wish to become as selfless as they. In either case, we owe our successful training to our encounters with all sentient beings and therefore feel gratitude towards them. Because they allow us to cultivate virtues, sentient beings are the direct cause of the perfect state of enlightenment. They are the immediate requisites for us to break free of samsara. Indeed, we should feel very grateful towards them. Reflect on the fact that those who appear to cause you harm are not really harming you. They are helping you to see that the real cause of harm is you, your own ego. Without ego there can be no harm. These are the instructions to embark on the path of awakening by transforming adversities with conventional bodhicitta.

Additionally, here I will add that a mind full of virtues reaps the excellent harvest of the bodhisattva bhumis. The ten bhumis are the extraordinary levels of realization of mind. By accomplishing them we will ultimately be free of samsara and attain Buddhahood.

The second extraordinary instruction is how ultimate bodhicitta is used to transform adversities into the path of awakening:
Cultivate deluded appearance as the Four Kayas; emptiness is the unsurpassed protection.

"Deluded appearance" refers to the fact that all the suffering and obstacles that are experienced are illusions, the deluded activity of a dualistic mind. When you really examine the negative or bad things that happen, you will clearly see that they are all like a dream. Using the techniques you have to analyze the empty nature of all phenomena and directly apply mindfulness to all experience, apply them to the sensations you experience as bad. You will discover that these so-called bad experiences are the most useful to help you recognize the unborn nature of mind. Just as a small fire can quickly burn a large stack of hay, a bad feeling or experience, once analyzed, will effectively and quickly help you to understand the unborn nature of everything. A really good Mind Training practitioner who is in deep meditation will find even a disturbing ghost to be his or her number one helper. A disturbing ghost can do things like push you, call your name, cause you to experience discomfort or nausea. In short, they will provide you with many disturbances. When that happens, apply all your skills of analysis and direct mindfulness to it. You will undoubtedly come to the conclusion that everything that is experienced is nothing but mind. After some time, you will have absolute confidence and a totally relaxed mind. With that comes the spontaneous realization of the unborn nature of mind. In this way, each and every adversity can be used on the path to awakening, and with this realization you will also see that in fact every adversity—when it is recognized as unborn—carries the truth nature, the dharmakaya.

The dharmakaya is one of four bodies, or kayas, of

the Buddha. These four kayas are the four ways in which enlightenment manifests. If we think of them in relation to a Buddha, they can be described as follows: the dharmakaya, or body of truth nature, is the timeless awakened wisdom of a Buddha, his purified mind; the sambhogakaya, or body of fulfilling joy, is a spectacular light form of the Buddha that is only perceived by highly accomplished practitioners; the nirmanakaya, or wish-fulfilling body, is the flesh and blood body of a Buddha that all living beings can perceive; and the svabhavika-kaya, the essence body, is the totality of the three. If we think of them in the context of how awakening manifests as the nature of mind, we can add to this description: the dharmakaya or body of truth nature, can also be understood as the unborn nature of mind; sambhogakaya or body of fulfilling joy, can also be understood as the unobstructed nature of mind; nirmanakaya or wish-fulfilling body, can also be understood as the nonabiding nature of mind; and svabhavikakaya, the totality and inseparability of the first three.

In fact, if you examine the illusions of deluded appearance you will find that they have the nature of unborn dharmakaya. Their quality of unobstructedness shows that they have the nature of sambhogakaya. Further, they are not trapped in the workings of dualistic conceptualization. This freedom from conceptualization demonstrates their natural flexibility and demonstrates the

quality of nirmanakaya. Finally, all three kayas share
one nature; that is the svabhavikakaya, and the nature of
the svabhavikakaya is emptiness.

One who is able to enter a state of meditation such
that they experience deluded appearance as the four
kayas is protected by emptiness. Emptiness is, in fact,
the unsurpassable protection. The best example of this is
when Shakyamuni was under the Bodhi tree on the very
verge of enlightenment. Mara, the tempter, was so determined to prevent Shakyamuni's success that he came
with his armies and tried to destroy the physical body
of the Buddha-to-be. Because Shakyamuni profoundly
understood emptiness, that insight protected him and
Mara's arrows fell to the ground before him as a harm-
less rain of flowers. Of course he was nearly a Buddha
at the time, dwelling on the 10th bhumi, so this is not
applicable to every practitioner's situation. We may draw
a different example from the life of Milarepa, however,
from when he was still relatively new to the path. One
day after gathering firewood he returned to his cave to
find five round-eyed demons waiting there for him. His
first thought was to appease them, so made them offerings and praised them in the hopes that they would be
satisfied and go away, but they proceeded to attack him.
Then he invoked a wrathful deity to conquer them, but
they became even more enraged. Finally he invoked the
power of emptiness, really meditating profoundly on the

nature of emptiness: *I have already fully realized that all beings and all phenomena are of one's own mind. And the mind itself is emptiness. What is the use of all these efforts! How foolish I am to try to physically dispel these demons and trouble-makers!* And with that utterance and realization, the demons were dispelled. Milarepa had to work hard to apply the remedy of emptiness, whereas for the Buddha it occurred quite spontaneously. But the cause is the same: realization of emptiness. Therefore it is the supreme, unsurpassable protection.

Three views are like the treasury of the sky, the unsurpassed protection of the yoga.

When you implement bodhicitta on adversities you should develop and maintain three views that will alter your perspective profoundly and enable you to cut through the obstacles of hope and doubt. The three views are: happiness, gratitude, and purity.

Happiness: Adversities that may at first seem harmful are in fact the complete opposite. They are extremely helpful. Obstacles and disturbances are actually reminders to you that you have not perfected the two bodhicittas. Be happy that you now have a clear reminder to work on your bodhicitta.

Gratitude: Understand that adversities warn us to not be too relaxed, to not let our precious human life be taken for granted. We must use this precious life for the ultimate goal of awakening and not waste time on other things. If we misuse this opportunity now, we may fall into darkness for eons. In this way, adversities are as kind as parents to us. Therefore, you may go so far as to feel love for adversities, for they prevent you from misusing your precious human life.

Purity: Think about how as a result of every obstacle and harm in your life, you may develop the greatest results from meditation. This type of harm is therefore not harmful at all. It is, rather, full of remarkable qualities like a very bitter medicine that will completely cure your sickness. It is therefore completely pure, as pure as the most effective medicine.

Keeping these three views will protect your practice and allow you to develop from everything that happens. Maintaining these three views of happiness, gratitude and purity will create and multiply merit as vast as the sky, enough to fill a treasury as limitless as the size of the sky. With this vast store of merit, the result is that you will spontaneously help sentient beings for countless eons.

"Yoga" is a complex word with many meanings. In this context, it is appropriate to examine how the term is used in Tibetan. The Tibetan word for yoga is *neljor* (*rnal "byor*). "Nel" is the original awakened nature of mind, the dharmakaya or truth nature. "Jor" is a verb that means to reach or attain. "Neljor", therefore, means to reach the original nature of mind. It is protection because for as long as you maintain this practice, you can implement the three views to overcome any obstacle. Meditation manuals explain it this way: when water is absorbed into the air, water comes out. Like clouds and rain. In that way, you can say that water is removed by water. Each and every obstacle on your path, each and every harm suffered along the way, will in fact cause obstacles and harm to disappear. In that way, implementing the three views protects you from all obstacles.

The third is the extraordinary instruction to
convert adversities into the path of awakening:
Mastering the four practices is the supreme method.

The four noble practices are: develop the cause of happiness; abandon the cause of suffering; make use of harm from others; and bring help from the positive and powerful nonhuman living beings. By employing them you will swiftly learn to turn all experiences into positive ones.

Develop the cause of happiness: Happiness only comes from the right cause: merit, the fruit of generosity and other virtues. For example, knowing that generosity creates the cause of happiness, you embrace the spirit of generosity in your intentions, actions, and wishes. Whenever something good comes your way, you give and share it with others. Whenever you wish for something good to happen to you, concurrently wish the same for others as well. The result is the accumulation of incalculable merit and happiness both now and in the future.

Abandon the cause of suffering: There is not one sentient being who wishes to suffer. The cause of suffering is all non-virtuous activities. Therefore, simply refrain from them:

Physical non-virtuous activities: Refrain from all acts that harm others such as killing, stealing directly or indirectly the property of others, and sexual misconduct.

Verbal non-virtuous activities: Refrain from all negative speech such as slander, lies, deceit, manipulation, as well as wild, loose talk.

Mental non-virtuous activities: Refrain from negative states of mind like envy, harmful thoughts, and wrong views.

Make use of harm from others: The "others" in this case are ghosts or spirits who may cause you disturbances and obstructions. Prepare a suitable feast according to the desire filled illusions of the millions of ghosts. Mentally multiply your offerings as much as possible, and then offer them to the ghosts:

From the combined power of my conventional and ultimate bodhicitta, I encourage all ghosts to engender the mind of loving kindness and devotion to the Three Jewels.

Please enjoy this feast. May your hunger be satisfied and your feelings of envy and jealousy be purified.

I am on the path of the noble dharma practice. Please contribute to my success through either helping me or harming me. Your harm will help me to accomplish my practice of patience and will cause me to increase my compassion ever more for all beings in the lower realms. Additionally, any service and support you give me will be most appreciated.

Bring help from the positive and powerful nonhuman living beings: Again, arrange a splendid feast of offerings for the positive nonhuman beings in accordance with their illusions. Multiply the offerings as much as possible in your mind. This is based in your bodhicitta, your deep wish to fulfill the needs of all other beings. Wish to make all these beings very happy and in return, ask them to support you in your dharma practice for the benefit of all sentient beings.

Whatever you encounter in the present, use it in your meditation.

Implement the Mind Training methods on every situation you encounter during the day. Good or bad, you can make it meaningful and useful to your practice.

When you are happy, comfortable, and things are going smoothly for you, you should know that it is the ripening of good karma sown in the past. If you just enjoy and grasp at the many pleasures as much as you can, then very soon your good karma will run out. Like suffering, good fortune also passes.

You can still engender bodhicitta when you are happy. Recollect that all sentient beings must also be happy: *I wish to give sentient beings the same good conditions that I have. May they be happy, too.* Through this wish and through actual giving and sharing with others, you are multiplying the positive causes and merit. In this way, the causes for happiness for beings everywhere are ever increasing.

Similarly, in the face of any terrible situation, continue to train in lojong. Instead of feeling lost, angry, or fearful, use the ordeal to practice tonglen, giving and taking. Engender bodhicitta as you suffer. Take onto yourself all unhappiness from everyone. In effect, you are turning your difficulty into a precious opportunity to practice Mind Training.

Many yogis, like Milarepa, used to go around singing songs. They sang songs when they were happy:

> *Oh, I am happy. Very good, it means I can give.*
> *May all my happiness go to all sentient beings*
> *and let them enjoy!*

They sang songs when they were sad:

Oh, I am suffering. Very good, it means I can take. May I absorb the suffering of all sentient beings, and relieve them completely!

The yogis deployed the Mind Training methods all day and all night long. Consequently, they experienced no problems whatsoever.

As your practice of Mind Training matures, you will feel your freedom expand increasingly. The usual walls of desire and aversion will begin to break down. Whatever happens to you, good or bad, will no longer make any difference to you. You will be open to anything because you can turn it all into the path of awakening.

THE FOURTH POINT

Implement Mind Training in this Life

The Fourth Point:
Implement Mind Training in this life.

This fourth point condenses the key instructions of Mind Training into the practice of the five powers in life and the five powers at death.

The instructions condensed into their essence:
Train in the five powers.

To enhance and accelerate your progress in Mind Training, you should train and develop these five powers in your daily life:

The power of resolution: Resolve that from now on, you make it an imperative to develop and strengthen your bodhicitta. You are determined that your bodhicitta will never diminish, that it will only increase. You act to benefit others and you will practice meditation to fully develop the wisdom of ultimate bodhicitta.

The power of familiarization: By being constantly mindful of the Mind Training instructions, you become familiar with them. Later, you will naturally apply them in daily life. Your lojong training will then carry on quite spontaneously, not only while you are awake but even as you sleep at night. This is what is meant by the power of familiarization.

The power of virtuous seed: bodhicitta is the powerful, virtuous seed. Any act that stems from this seed is very meritorious - for example, generosity.

Generosity simply means to give. Protecting, offering assistance, and teaching others about the dharma are all acts of generosity. When you share anything that is good and useful with others, you will quickly accumulate positive merit.

Merit is like the most superb fertilizer for a field, and what grows in this field is bodhicitta. Then the merit from bodhicitta multiplies exponentially and the positive cycle continues.

When your merit is strong you will be able to accomplish positive activities you could not achieve before. Then you dedicate the resultant merit again to benefit others. In this way, your store of merit will ever multiply and your positive activities ever increase.

From now on, you should not hesitate to benefit others. Every kindness is worth your while, be it even as tiny an act as feeding small birds and animals. As much as possible, you should share and give support to others sincerely without any reservation.

The power of renouncing the ego: The greatest obstacle to bodhicitta is ego clinging. Where there is ego, bodhicitta is absent. Ego is the source of all selfish actions and thoughts. It creates nothing but negative karma and it destroys your good karma.

As soon as self-clinging appears, recognize it and fight it off. During the twelve hours of the day and twelve hours of the night, firmly resist the dictates of the ego. You have to keep reminding yourself that you will not be taken over. In time, that firm resolve to ignore the ego will become your nature.

The power of wishes: Make as many wishes that are beneficial to sentient beings as you can. Dedicate any merit, however small, by wishing that sentient beings meet with good circumstances and conditions.

The Buddhas and bodhisattvas are our models. The Buddhas" tremendous powers to help sentient beings come from a cause: the wishes they have made for beings from the moment they engendered bodhicitta until their enlightenment. All wishes come to fruition upon enlightenment, and therefore the Buddhas" wishes for us are happening now. This is the power of wishes.

The Great Vehicle teachings on death are the five powers themselves; your conduct is critical.

The teachings on transferring the mind at the moment

of death, *phowa*, are for advanced practitioners who have reached a certain level of competency in their meditation. However, the following five powerful causes at death capture the essence of phowa.

When you are about to die, you should specifically engage these five causes. They will support you in the bardo (the intermediate state between death and rebirth). In addition, you should also follow the advice on the physical posture for dying.

Powerful white seed: "White" here means positive, and the one positive root is bodhicitta. Therefore, take the Bodhisattva Vow again in case you have damaged any of its commitments.

As you die, relinquish all attachment to your belongings and relationships alike. Make sure that you do not have any regrets or worries.

In order to be completely carefree and unattached to anything at death you have to prepare for it. You should make a will in advance and give clear instructions regarding the care of your dependents, making sure to seek the consent of people you trust to look after their welfare after your demise.

As to the distribution of your possessions, specify how you would like them to be divided among different individuals or organizations. The point is to settle your affairs beforehand so you can feel mentally free at the actual time of dying.

When possible, you can make donations to two kinds of charities: those that provide temporary help to the underprivileged in the form of hospitals, social services, food and shelters; and those that provide the ultimate help of dharma. Choose to support either one or both.

It is important that you do not cling to anything as you die. Clinging disturbs your mind. The worst scenario is that you find yourself thinking about how to settle everything at the time of death. Your mind will then follow that train of thought into the bardo and that might bring dire consequences for you.

Powerful prayer: Dying wishes are very powerful. Therefore, at that time, invite all the Buddhas and bodhisattvas before you and make supplications to them. From your mind, pay respect to all the great beings, the Buddhas, bodhisattvas, arhats, and pratyekabuddhas. Request their blessings and the support of their wishes to make your wishes come true and your wishes should all be channeled towards obtaining a good rebirth, one where you will be very beneficial to beings. It is recommended that you recite Samantabhadra's wishing prayer as much as possible.

Powerful connecting cause in the bardo: The connecting cause is bodhicitta in both of its aspects, conventional and ultimate. Just before death, you should fully embrace bodhicitta. Hold good wishes for sentient beings in your mind while at the same time continuing to embrace the wisdom of ultimate bodhicitta. Try not to be over-whelmed by the bardo illusions and remember to apply the view that all phenomena are illusions.

Powerful suppression of the ego: Any negative thought or feeling due to self-centeredness must be sup-pressed. You should have no doubt that self-clinging will create only negative causes. If possible, try to recognize the empty nature of the self, the view of ultimate bodh-icitta. Do not get angry at anything because anger drives away bodhicitta, and do not get entangled in disturbing emotions.

Powerful habit: Compassion is a powerful mental habit. Just as you have trained during your life to engen-der it as much as possible, as you are dying, summon up all your compassion for sentient beings. Call to mind the feeling of loving kindness towards them and allow the feeling to expand. Do not doubt what is about to happen and do not hope for good results either. Simply remain in bodhicitta.

Bodhicitta will bless your entire mind and that bless-ing will continue after your death. There, in the bardo, it will carry you in a direction exactly according to your wish. This is the way to be reborn as a bodhisattva. As soon as you are reborn, your mind will be connected to bodhicitta and in that life you will be very helpful and useful to others.

Physical Posture for Dying

The "one position" refers to the posture most favorable for a dying person. As you die, the top part of your head should face north. You should lie on your right side with your head on a pillow. Your right palm should be under your cheek and your legs straight, if possible. As well, your left arm should be straight and placed over your hip. Look at pictures of the Buddha when he was dying (the so-called "sleeping Buddha") and copy him.

THE FIFTH POINT

The Measure of Mind Training

Fifth Point: The Measure of Mind Training.

This fifth point gives you the yardstick to gauge your progress in practice. The best evidence of success in lojong is when you can spontaneously use whatever it is that you are doing to subdue self-clinging. When that arises naturally and effortlessly, it is a true sign that you have accomplished the results of lojong. In other words, Mind Training has become your nature. At this point, great wisdom will shine spontaneously and as naturally as the light of the sun grows from dawn to noon.

All dharma teachings are for a single purpose.

The Buddha taught the dharma for one purpose: to diminish self-clinging. When you are no longer absorbed by self-concern, that is the first measure of success in lojong.

Successful practitioners *know* differently than others. They naturally know whether ego is dominating or not, whether it is increasing, diminishing, or remaining the same. For them, Mind Training has become a habit of mind and the ego is in check. As soon as an obstacle appears due to self-clinging, it is recognized and not followed. A non-practitioner cannot imagine having that kind of awareness let alone trying to control self-clinging.

Free of self-clinging, successful practitioners have few worries. They feel comfortable, peaceful, and at ease with themselves and others. As your practice matures, you will experience and recognize these liberating effects by yourself. You will not need confirmation from your teacher or from anyone else.

Rely on the better of the two witnesses.

In general, we speak of two witnesses: self and others. Always rely on yourself as the chief witness. You know whether you are training and abiding by the vows and commitments. Only you know the impact Mind Training has on you and on how you conduct yourself.

The methods ground you in perfect motivation and the training guides you towards perfect behavior. Therefore when you are naturally and effortlessly acting properly it means your practice is successful. You will have no regrets. In fact, you will experience deep satisfaction.

Be sustained continuously by a joyful mind.

It is a good sign if you are sustained by a constantly happy mind. Even when confronted by obstacles you are able to use them to train yourself. Because of the powerful merit accumulated practicing Mind Training, great happiness will develop in your mind. When you experience this result you should neither be overly excited, nor worry if the happiness goes away. You should not care for it at all. Instead, continue to maintain a clear and stable mind, a state of equanimity, and gradually you will be sustained continuously by a joyful mind.

You are well trained if you can even withstand distraction.

In the moment of a negative thought or disturbance, if you can maintain your composure and naturally apply the methods to subdue it without feeling any strain, then this means you are well trained. The correction is quite automatic owing to your proficiency in practice. Even in the midst of an upheaval, you can remain composed and continue to use the immediate conditions to train. Like an expert rider, you won't fall off the horse even when distracted.

Being stable in your practice does not mean that you no longer have any self-grasping. Rather, it means that when it does surface it is remedied right away. Naropa once said to Marpa,

> *"Your practice has attained to such a level*
> *that, like a coiled snake, you are able to*
> *release yourself in an instant."*

It will be evident that you have accomplished your practice when the **five great qualities of mind** arise:

Bodhicitta: The first great mind is bodhicitta. The effect of a dominant and pervasive bodhicitta mind is a complete feeling of satisfaction. While you continue to train, your contentment is so strong that you have no desire for anything else.

Great taming: Your mind is so tame that you notice the tiniest mistake which creates a negative cause and correct it immediately.

Great patience: You have enormous patience to subdue your negative emotions and defilements. You have no reservation whatsoever when it comes to dealing with a negative state of mind. In other words, you continue to train your mind no matter what.

Great merit: When everything you do, say, or think comes from one intention—to benefit others—then you are one with the dharma practice. Simultaneously, as you perform your daily practice and affairs, merit is accumulating continuously. That, in turn, directly supports your positive activities generating ever more merit. In this way, great merit multiplies automatically.

Great yoga: The great yoga (practice) is ultimate bodhicitta. It is the vast and profound mind of wisdom that exposes the nature of reality. To possess and sustain this perfect view is thus the quintessential dharma practice.

Through Mind Training you will achieve these five great qualities of mind. You have to earnestly train to develop them as they will not come about through wishful thinking.

The arising of the five great minds will prove that the essence of the bodhisattva practice has become your nature. You will not engage in any negativity no matter how small. You are in control and cannot be swayed by negative emotions. For you, all the remedies go into operation quite automatically even when you are not paying too much attention. As the remedies are being applied, you remain calm and balanced. Most of your time is naturally spent working for others or for your enlightenment (which is also, in effect, for sentient beings).

One very important point is this: true compassion is not emotional. Mature practitioners have a clear view grounded in ultimate bodhicitta. They already know the nature of suffering itself. Their compassion is influenced by wisdom so there is no sadness or emotion involved. Unhampered and free of emotions, bodhisattvas help others in a sensible and appropriate way.

Commitments of Mind Training

Sixth Point: Commitments of Mind Training.

The sixth point lists the fifteen precepts of Mind Training. With the exception of the first precept (which provides broad guidelines), they spell out the behavior you should shun in daily life, mistakes which will spoil your efforts and progress in practice.

Always abide by the three basic principles.

The three basic principles guard you from mistakes:

Keep your commitments and vows: they include the two unsurpassed vows of Refuge and Bodhisattva, and these Mind Training precepts. Do not overlook or disregard even the slightest of transgressions.

In order to succeed in subduing self-clinging, do not overindulge in anything including your self-image. Don't try to stand out or make an impression that you are someone different or special, either overtly or subtly.

Be equally patient with everything: your patience should not be selective. For example, you should not choose to be patient only with your friends but not with your enemies. That is biased patience.

Remaining natural, transform your attitude.

The normal attitude of living beings is selfishness. "Transform your attitude" means you should not be selfish. At the same time, don't show off your efforts to change. How you care for others need not be displayed for everyone to see. You should neither show how you have changed, nor how good you are at it. That is the way of charlatans.

Do not talk about the defects of others.

In your speech, do not make fun, tease, or bring attention to what you see as a physical defect or handicap in others.

Whatever the faults of others may be, do not contemplate them.

It is best to think about the strengths and good qualities of others. Do not think about the shortcomings of others. In other words, do not have any opinion about their missteps.

Abandon poisonous food.

Just as food should not be poisoned, dharma practice should also not be contaminated. Guard your practice against ego-clinging which produces negative emotions. Check your inner agenda to filter out all self-serving interests.

Helping others is not based on returning favors.

This commitment is a culturally specific one appropriate to Tibetan people during the time of Atisha. Especially among the nobles, there was a tendency to do good or harm to others based on how they had treated you in the past. If someone had treated you badly, you would remember that harm and return it at some point in the future. Likewise, if someone had done something kind for you, you would behave kindly towards that person as a kind of payback. This commitment is designed to ensure that helping others is done out of a genuine sense of compassion and love, and not a sense of duty. Doing good for others must not depend on how well or badly that person has treated you in the past.

Do not expose the faults of others to irritate them.

If someone attempts to provoke an argument or a fight by attacking you either directly with aggressive words or actions, or indirectly with sarcasm or by some other means, you must not respond in kind.

Do not wait in ambush.

Do not wait for an opportunity to strike back at those against whom you hold a grudge. Never seek revenge.

Never strike at the heart.

Do not be mean and do not make life or situations difficult for others. You should not be sadistic or cruel to others.

Do not put an ox's load on a cow.

Do not overburden or put undue pressure on someone else. Do not shirk your own responsibilities or abuse your authority by passing your work or problems onto others either directly or through crafty manipulation.

Do not aim to be the best.

Do not aim to win or to rise above others. Do not try to get a better deal for yourself at the expense of others.

Do not misuse the remedy.

Do not misuse the purpose of dharma practice, specifically here Mind Training practice. The merit from it should be dedicated for the future. The fruition of merit is not to enable you to enjoy a life of luxury, fame, and esteem in the here and now. Rather, dedicate all your merit to supporting your service to others in the future. For example, making wishes for your own future wealth, for your own good health or to escape from harmful ghosts is a waste of merit.

Do not use gods for evil.

In this context, "god" is a metaphor for anything related to religion. Throughout history, religion has been exploited for personal gain and ambition. Today, this misuse is still happening. People use religion to enhance their egos and negative emotions, to boost their self-image and pride rather than to develop humility and patience. On a smaller scale, people use it to gain material goods. On a larger scale, they use religion politically to secure leadership roles and to control the populace.

Religion can also be misused in other ways. Deities that are meant to help and liberate you can be misused, causing them to be harmful for others. For example, if you invoke a protective deity to curse an enemy, you are making that wrathful deity evil by using him or her in that way. I will add here that whether or not such a deity really exists is not the point—the intention is wrong and harmful.

Be like a humble servant before all.

With the adoption of Mind Training, you are renouncing former goals you may have had, such as to become famous or powerful. You must not behave as though you are special or superior to others, since you have also renounced the view that others are less important than yourself. Therefore you must be humble, as humble as the lowest servant before everyone.

Do not delight in the suffering of others.

Do not wish harm or death on an enemy, or wish to profit from the downfall of someone. You shouldn't hunt animals for pleasure, for example. This point also includes wishing someone would die, disappear, or suffer harm so you might inherit material things, gain status in society, or get promoted in an organization.

Concluding Remarks:

Your only aim from now on is to achieve enlightenment

for the sake of sentient beings and therefore nothing else is important. A true practitioner abandons everything and has nothing left to do in his or her life except for working towards enlightenment. For example, during his many years of practice, people thought Milarepa was insane and they continuously said so. Milarepa didn't care, and why should he? We should all strive to follow the example of his single-pointed dedication to his goal.

THE SEVENTH POINT

Advice for Mind Training

The Seventh Point: Advice for Mind Training

The seventh point consists of twenty-two suggestions to support and enhance the practice of Mind Training.

Practice all yogas in one way.

There are yogas (practices) for specific daily functions such as eating, sleeping, walking, sitting, and dressing. All of them can be covered under one essential practice: whatever it is that you are doing, do it with the wish that it will bring benefit to beings. It is simple. For example, if you are walking up some stairs, you can think: *I wish to take all sentient beings up these steps of dharma to enlightenment.* If you go to a beautiful park, think *I wish to bring all sentient beings to Nirvana from suffering!*

Subdue all obstacles by one method.

Whatever difficulty you encounter, practice tonglen (giving and taking). Think: *Through my problem, may*

I relieve the obstacles of all sentient beings. May I take all their problems onto myself so that they may be happy and obstacle free.

Sometimes advanced practitioners may encounter small obstacles or difficulties, such as ill health, for brief periods. These are signs that the bad karma is clearing up, a side effect of proper practice, as it were. The specific kinds of problems depend entirely on the individual. If you find yourself at this stage, rest assured that it is a good sign. Continue to apply the methods to the obstacles. The point is not to get thrown off by hardships. Do not be alarmed that they are happening to you.

**Two actions to perform:
at the beginning and at the end.**

When you wake up in the morning, think: *I will seriously practice Mind Training this whole day.* At night, before you fall asleep, you should think: *as I sleep, may my mind abide in the practice.* Because the accumulation of merit depends entirely on your motivation, even as you sleep the merit will accumulate automatically.

Be patient with whichever of the two arises.

Patience is a universally recognized virtue so you should always be patient. The two conditions that arise are *posi-*

tive and *negative*. First, when you are happy and comfortable, be patient and don't overindulge. Second, when you are downtrodden, you should feel neither afraid nor overwhelmed. Be patient and learn to moderate yourself under both favorable and unfavorable conditions.

Guard the two even at the cost of your life.

The first of the two refers to the general vows and commitments of the Bodhisattva Vehicle such as the Refuge and Bodhisattva vows. The second is the essence of Mind Training. The best way to protect these two is not to commit any of the transgressions listed under the sixth point of Mind Training. Do not underestimate their importance and value. From time to time, review them point by point.

Train in the three difficulties.

When we deal with negative emotions we encounter three difficulties.

The first is learning to recognize the negative emotion when it first appears. It is often difficult to notice it right away. You have to hone your mindfulness, otherwise once the appearance of an emotion has escaped your attention, it takes form in many thoughts and feelings.

To subdue the emotion is the second difficulty. You

have to apply the appropriate remedy and not follow the emotional effects.

The third difficulty is to ensure that the negativity will not continue—that it will not happen again. This means to eventually uproot self-clinging, the source of all emotions. In order to achieve this goal, practice the dharma methods to develop wisdom.

You have to practice dealing with all three difficulties. Of the three, the most important is to try to tame each negative emotion as soon as you notice it. Once you have developed the habit of controlling your mind, these three will cease to be difficulties at all.

Keep the three main causes.

Here, "causes" refers to the causes of successful Mind Training.

The first main cause of success in lojong or in any dharma practice is a qualified spiritual teacher who can teach and guide you.

Second, you must train. Once you have received the proper instructions from a qualified teacher, work hard to become competent in the methods. All dharma methods tame the mind. Even though people generally think that a horse is trained by its trainer, in truth it is really the horse that learns to calm itself.

The third cause encompasses all the materials and

conditions necessary to sustain your practice. For example, you should have adequate food, shelter, and the basic necessities.

Cultivate the three without diminishment.

First, your respect for your spiritual teacher must not diminish. A true spiritual teacher helps you in earnest to attain enlightenment without ever deviating from the genuine dharma. People who are acting or pretending to be teachers while harboring selfish interests and ambitions are mere charlatans.

Second, dharma practice is very important so your zeal to practice must not dwindle. Your enthusiasm in turn hinges on how well you understand the profound meaning; that is to say, the deeper your understanding of the dharma, the greater your appreciation and commitment to practice will be.

Third, your efforts to abide by the vows and precepts must not diminish. Do not be lax in your attention to the risk of committing any of the downfalls of Mind Training. The commitments you make protect the quality of your practice. Be vigilant in how you conduct yourself in order to uphold every vow you have undertaken.

Make the three inseparable.

Our body, speech, and mind should be engaged in positive and beneficial activities. Physically, you should do prostrations and other dharma practice as much as possible. Verbally you can engage in positive activities by reciting sutras, prayers such as Samantabhadra's wishing prayer, and making limitless wishes to benefit sentient beings. Mentally, you can continually embrace bodhicitta, the essential motivation.

Practice with impartiality.

You should not discriminate against people based on their sex, race, country of origin, status, or beliefs, etc. You should similarly hold no bias or prejudice against anything. Implement the Mind Training methods equally on everyone and in every circumstance.

All training must be pervasive and profound.

Train thoroughly so that the essence of Mind Training takes root in the depths of your mind. Express it genuinely through your thoughts, speech, and actions. It is not enough to verbalize the Mind Training instructions since that is not useful to anyone.

Meditate consistently in every circumstance.

Normally people avoid difficulties. However, for Mind Training practice, you should use everything you encounter—even problematic situations—to train yourself.

Do not depend on external conditions.

You do not need to rely on any other method but Mind Training. Make use of adverse conditions to train yourself as you don't need outer conditions to be perfect in order to practice Mind Training. Your efforts will definitely pay off and your practice will quickly mature.

From now on, practice is the chief priority.

All seven points of Mind Training concur on this point: practice now. Do not wait for the perfect time to practice. When you encounter bad conditions, breathe in and take on the suffering of all others. When you encounter good conditions, breathe out and send them off to others. It is as simple as that.

Among all the lives that you have had, this one is the most important because you have obtained a precious human birth. Therefore, you should make it meaningful.

Among all the opportunities you meet in this life,

meeting with the *dharma* is the greatest. You must therefore not waste or misuse your chance now.

Among the two general *dharma* practices of academic study or meditation practice, you should follow the second.

Among the many methods of practice, lojong is the most important of all. Therefore, you should practice Mind Training now.

Do not be misdirected.

Do not be misdirected in the virtues:

Misdirected patience: You have no patience to practice the meaningful dharma, but when it comes to activities that will pull you down to the lower realms you have a lot of patience.

Misdirected intention: Any intention or wish to gain pleasure for this life only is misdirected intention.

Misdirected enjoyment: When you do not enjoy abiding by the dharma and creating positive causes, and instead you take pleasure in amoral conduct and activities, that is misdirected enjoyment.

Misdirected pity: Misdirected pity is when you feel sorry for people who are practicing the dharma or benefiting others. You pity them, thinking that they are missing out on life. Or, you feel sorry for people who are spending their money on charities and the dharma instead of on themselves. There is a good example of this from Milarepa's life. When his sister found him meditating in isolation in his mountain cave, without clothing, food or any disciples, she felt terribly sorry for him and told him that he didn't even appear to be human any more. She cried at the sight of her brother in such a state. This is a clear example of misdirected pity[1].

Misdirected focus: When you direct people towards what is only of temporary benefit in this life rather than the ultimate benefit that the dharma affords, that is misdirected focus.

Misdirected rejoicing: Misdirected rejoicing is when you cheer someone on as a hero when he or she is actually engaging in harmful activities and creating negative karma. That is misdirected rejoicing. For example, thinking, *He's so smart...he cheated so many people, and made so much money!*

This discussion is of *misdirected virtues* and does not apply to the use of skillful means—skillfully employing unusual methods—by bodhisattvas. An example of using skillful means is when the Buddha used music to tame the king of one of the god realms. Knowing that to tame the king would tame all the gods of his realm, and knowing that the king loved music, the Buddha manifested to him as a great musician and they played music

---

[1] The Tibetan word translated here as "pity" is nyingje (snying rje), which in this context means "pity" and not compassion.

together. The Buddha skillfully taught the king of the gods the dharma in that way. In such a case, this is not misdirected virtue.

Do not be inconsistent.

You should practice steadily with regularity. Avoid going from one extreme to the other, as in practicing a lot sometimes and hardly at all at other times. Encourage yourself regularly. Be steadfast in your practice and your success is guaranteed. You all know the story of the tortoise and the hare. Be the tortoise!

Train uninterruptedly.

Train uninterruptedly in Mind Training until it becomes your nature.

Liberate by examination and analysis.

Analysis means having two minds—the observing mind and the observed. In the beginning, examine your own mind regularly as a form of self-analysis. Determine which negative states are more dominant in you. It is important to understand that their triggers are within you. Complete your analysis by knowing the appropriate remedies to apply. Then, with practice, you will eventually be able to liberate yourself from the negative mental states.

When your practice is stable the defilements are recognized more spontaneously. The appropriate remedy automatically appears when the negativity appears. This is considered a very good result.

Do not seek recognition.

Do not expect rewards, recognition, or appreciation from people you have helped. You should not expect them to return your favors. You should also not go bragging to everyone about what you have done. Bodhisattvas do not expect any recognition or rewards whatsoever.

Do not hold on to anger.

When people have offended you or hurt you, don't hold on to the anger and remember the wrong done to you.

Supplemental commentary: *This particular advice is especially applicable for Tibetans. It is because in Tibetan culture, children are encouraged from a young age to remember the wrong done them as a form of self-protection. Tibetans who can remember every harm suffered are praised for being strong. Even lamas who are in political circles have this negative disposition. Needless to say, this is* *totally against Buddhist teachings. To eliminate this kind of cultural conditioning, Buddhist masters emphasize the importance of not holding onto one's anger and not holding grudges.*

Do not be moody.

In Buddhist ethics, it is considered a character flaw to live and behave "like the weather". Irritable people are always changing and not steadfast in their commitments and goals. Their interest in things is usually short-lived. For example, an irritable, flighty person might move from teacher to teacher, or change his or her practice all the time. He or she is unable to settle down long enough to learn things properly, making him or her a poor candidate for dharma practice.

Do not seek gratitude.

Whatever it is that you do in the dharma, do not expect praise, thanks, rewards, or recognition from others.

Conclusion

The author explains that now he has the necessary confidence and will to encourage others:

Through my great intention and resolve,
I ignored my own suffering and ill repute,
and obtained the instructions to defeat my own ego
clinging. Now, I have no regrets even if I were to die
this moment.
— Chekawa Yeshé Dorjé

Ja Chekawa Yeshé Dorjé, the author of the root text of the Seven Points of Mind Training, concluded the root verses with this simple and concise verse. The fact that he had no regrets shows that Chekawa had achieved enlightenment and felt deep satisfaction. His achievement of the realization of a bodhisattva was indeed an extraordinary feat. He owed his success to the very Mind Training instructions he had sought after, obtained, and practiced.

Chekawa condensed the precious instructions and committed them to verse for us and for all sentient beings. The slogans encompass a profound teaching powerful enough to bring any committed practitioner to enlightenment within one lifetime, just as they did for him.

Sechilbupa was one of Chekawa's main disciples, and it was he who wrote down these instructions expressed in slogans. When he had finished, Chekawa announced that he would throw a tea party to celebrate the naming of the teachings as *The Seven Points of Mind Training*, and he did just that. Since then, his Seven Points of Mind Training have spread everywhere and have benefited many great masters.

Chekawa passed away in the female wood sheep year (1175 C.E.) at the age of 75 in a place called Ja Ngurmo in Central Tibet.

Final Remarks

This Mind Training practice is easy to learn, handy, and it includes all the profound meditation instructions. For a young person who has decided to give up all worldly pursuits and takes the time to practice in retreat this will be extremely beneficial. In fact, just this is enough for enlightenment. Even if you keep it to read over and over again, to instill the instructions in your mind, you are building great assets for your retirement! In fact, according to the Buddhist view of impermanence and karma, nobody knows when he or she will die. In any case, you cannot help but to recognize the fact that in this world it is not easy to do as you please and to do everything you want to. It is hard to find time for many things, we have to study when we are young, then look for a job to support ourselves and our families. But if you really engage with these teachings and try to train your mind, this is like the best savings for the future. For those who have already retired from their jobs, the teachings and practices contained in this book are my highest recommendation for you to meaningfully use the remainder of your precious human life. Whether you achieve enlightenment in one life like Chekawa Yeshé Dorjé, or after this life, or after many lives, this practice will carry you though as many lifetimes as it takes as a successful bodhisattva, free from the suffering of samsara, and finally enable you to achieve enlightenment.

Appendix

Glossary

arhat "worthy one" (Sanskrit). In Tibetan *trachompa* (sgra bcom pa) or "foe destroyer". The foes that have been destroyed are the afflictions. Arhats are a class of Buddhist saints, very highly realized practitioners and associated with the closest disciples of the Buddha.

Avalokiteshvara the name of the Bodhisattva of compassion. He can manifest as the deity of compassion but was also a monk, one of Buddha's disciples when he was teaching at Rajagriha.

bardo "intermediate state" (Tibetan). It generally refers to the intermediate state between death and rebirth, the experience of the mindstream at the time that one established life has passed and one is headed toward the next established life.

bhumi "stage, level, ground" (Sanskrit). It a technical term in discussion of the path of the bodhisattvas. There are ten bhumis in all, each of which is a level of attainment that culminates after the 10th bhumi with full awakening. The 10 are: Joyous, Stainless, Luminous, Radiant, Unconquerable, Manifest, Gone-Afar, Immovable, Good Wisdom, Dharma Cloud.

bodhi Awakening/enlightenment (Sanskrit).

bodhicitta "awakening mind" (Sanskrit). It is the altruistic intention, the mind bent on becoming awakened itself for the purpose of effectively relieving the suffering of others and guiding them to awakening.

bodhisattva "awakening being" (Sanskrit). A bodhisattva is a being who has dedicated himself or herself to achieving Awakening in order to benefit others. Every action of a bodhisattva is grounded in the altruistic intention (bodhicitta).

dharma a Sanskrit word with no literal translation. Usually it refers to the teachings of the Buddha (i.e. "I go for refuge to the dharma"). It is said to have eight meanings: knowledge, path, enlightenment, meritorious actions, life, doctrines, divination (anything that predicts the future), or a religious school.

dharmakaya see **kaya**

greatvehicle see **mahayana**

karma "action" (Sanskrit). It stands for *karman phalam*, "action and result", and refers to the profound truth of cause and effect.

kaya literally "body" (Sanskrit). There are said to be four bodies (kaya) of the Buddha, each of which expresses a different aspect of awakening. They range in their levels of subtlety and coarseness with respect to materiality. The **dharmakaya**, or **body of truth nature**, is the underlying truth nature of all phenomena. It is completely non-material. The **sambhogakaya**, or **body of fulfilling joy**, is a very subtle form that is visible only to very highly realized beings. It is a perfect body, displaying all signs of perfection, and its function is to bring joy and fulfillment to the beings who are able to perceive it. The *sambhogakaya* is the teacher of *bodhisattvas* on the 8th bhumi. The **nirmanakaya**, or **wish-fulfilling body**, is the physical body taken on by a Buddha. It appears through the force of a Buddha's compassion and is perceived by all ordinary beings as an ordinary being and is subject to birth, decay and death like all physical bodies. Finally, the **svabhavikakaya**, or **essence body**, is the totality of the first three.

lhaktong meditation of superior view (Tibetan). **Vipashyana** in Sanskrit. "Lhak" means supreme, and "tong" is experience. It is the experience of the supreme natural quality of mind.

mahabodhisattva see **bodhisattva**

mahayana "Great Vehicle" (Sanskrit). Mahayana is a particular form of Buddhism that employs the practice of skillful means (with great compassion as the method) and cultivates the wisdom that realizes the emptiness of self and all phenomena. .

nirmanakaya see **kaya**

nirvana "extinguished" (Sanskrit). The perfect goal of Buddhist practice, the extinction of all ignorance and all afflictions.

pratyekabuddha "solitary realizer" (Sanskrit). Pratyekabuddhas are those beings who have achieved enlightenment in human form but in a time when there is no Buddha. They have no teacher in their final life and gain enlightenment by remembering achievements from their past lives. In fact, one hundred eons before their enlightenment, their teacher was a Buddha and they accumulated merit by helping sentient beings for those one hundred eons. They help sentient beings by the very example of their own achievements.

sambhogakaya see **kaya**

samsara the round of rebirth (Sanskrit). Samsara is the endless cycle of rebirth characterized by suffering and delusion. Sentient beings are endlessly flung from one life to another by the force of their karma, ignorant of the causes of their own suffering and the potential to escape it.

Shakyamuni "The Sage of the Shakyas". "shakya" was the Prince Siddhartha's clan name. When he achieved awakening and became the Buddha he was known as Shakyamuni, the Sage of the Shakyas.

shamatha "calm abiding" (Sanskrit). **Shiné** in Tibetan. A type of meditation taught by the Buddha to train disciples to calm and pacify their minds.

shiné see shamatha

sutra All the direct teachings of the Buddha Shakyamuni are in the sutras. They contain the main doctrines of Buddhism.

svabhavikakaya see kaya

tantra "continuity". It is a continuity of awakened potential possessed by all. The teachings of tantra focus on how to transform one's own body, speech and mind into the body, speech and mind of the deity. It is a particular method for attaining enlightenment.

tonglen "giving and taking" (Tibetan). The profound meditation of giving all of one's good qualities to others and taking on all their suffering.

vipashyana see lhaktong

yoga "union" (Sanskrit). Neljor in Tibetan. Refers to any practice that unites the mind with its innate wisdom. "Nel" is the original awakened nature of mind, the *dharmakaya* or truth nature. "Jor" is a verb that means to reach or attain. "Neljor", therefore, means to reach the original nature of mind.

Bibliography

Chang, Garma C.C., trans. *The Hundred Thousand Songs of Milarepa*. Boston: Shambhala, 1962.

Jinpa, Thupten, trans. *Mind Training: the Great Collection*. Somerville: Wisdom Publications, 2006.

Kunga Rinpoche, Lama and Brian Cutillo, trans. *Drinking the Mountain Stream*. Boston: Wisdom, 1995.

Lhalungpa, Lobsang, trans. *The Life of Milarepa*. London: Penguin, 1979.

Rinpoche, Mipham. *mkhas pa'i tshul la 'jug pa'i sgo zhes bya ba'i bstan bcos bzhugs so (Gateway to Knowledge)*. trans. Erik Pema Kunsang. Hong Kong: Rangjung Yeshe Publications, 1997.

Shantideva. *byang chub sems dpa'i spyod pa la 'jug pa*. Sarnath: Vajra Vidya Institute. Library, 2004.

Index

A Note on the Type

This book was set in a digital version of Monotype Walbaum. The original typeface was created by Julius Erich Walbaum (1768–1839) in 1810. Before becoming a punch cutter with his own type foundries in Goslar and Weimer, he was apprenticed to a confectioner where he is said to have taught himself engraving, making his own cookie molds using tools made from sword blades. The letterforms were modeled on the "modern" cuts being made at the time by Giambattista Bodoni and the Didot family.

So here cometh
"Delphinium Books"
To recognize excellence in writing
And bring it to the attention
Of the careful reader
Being a book of the heart
Wherein is an attempt to body forth
Ideas and ideals for the betterment
Of men, eke women
Who are preparing for life
By living. . . .

(In the manner of Elbert Hubbard,
        "White Hyacinths," 1907)